A UNITED FRONT:
How to Help Your Spouse to Purity

setting CAPTIVES free

A UNITED FRONT

— How to Help Your Spouse to Purity —

Jody Cleveland

SETTING CAPTIVES FREE
PUBLISHING

Setting Captives Free Publishing
1400 W. Washington St., Ste. 104
Sequim, WA 98382

ISBN: 978-1-7337609-4-2
LCCN: 2019917371

Acknowledgements

*T*hank you, Jesus, for your eternal love displayed on the cross that saved me, sanctifies me, and compels me to share the hope of the gospel with others.

Thank you, my beloved husband, Mike, for your prayers, loving leadership, and patience, which have enabled me to share our story of healing and gospel reconciliation. I love you.

Thank you, Kaylee, Jeremy, Daniel, Joshua, Charity, and Joy; your love is a gift. I thank God for you.

Thank you to all my brothers and sisters at Setting Captives Free, who have spurred me on to love and good deeds by faithfully upholding the cross of Christ and His banner of love.

Table of Contents

Foreword

While we are not supposed to judge a book by its cover, we can judge a tree by its fruit. The book you are holding in your hands has produced very good fruit in the lives of countless women who have come to Setting Captives Free for help in their marriage.

For me, the fruit this book has produced is a little more personal. You might say that I, Jody's husband, am also the fruit that this book has produced. You see, I lived in unfaithfulness and impurity for many years of my life and our marriage, being captive to sin and the kingdom of darkness. But Jody's steadfast love and ongoing forgiveness of falls in the early days truly won my heart, which now belongs wholly to her, forever.

And isn't that how Jesus wins our hearts, too? He "took up our pain and bore our suffering…He was pierced for our transgressions; He was crushed for our iniquities…by His wounds, we are healed" (Isaiah 53:5). Yes, Jesus wins our hearts through love, the love that forgave even though He was crushed, the love that gave Himself even while He was suffering. Indeed, He has healed the entire church by His wounds.

And so, I'm not only Jesus' fruit, the fruit He bore when He, like a kernel of wheat, died and was put into the ground, but I'm also Jody's fruit. Like Jesus, she loved me even though I crushed her; she forgave me amid her suffering and, through the years of hurt, she continually pointed me to Jesus Christ and the truth of the gospel. That kind of love can break the hardest heart and mend the deepest wounds.

This book seems to contain the heart of my precious wife, wrapped up within its pages. I have watched her wrestle with the biblical text, beg God for His blessing on it, soak it in prayer, and wash it at the cross. I've seen her pour out herself as a drink offering in this book, giving not only the gospel of Jesus Christ but her own life. And so, you are holding two precious things in your hand: the powerful message of the cross, and the heart of my dear wife.

May Jody's heart and this message that has changed untold millions of lives throughout history, reach your heart and mend it by grace, and may your marriage experience the healing that Jody and I have.

—Mike Cleveland, Co-Founder of Setting Captives Free.

Introduction

*H*ello, my name is Jody Cleveland; welcome to the A United Front course. My husband, Mike, was enslaved to sexual impurity for many years before we experienced victory through the message of the cross and became a united front in our marriage. This course material is the fruit of what God worked into my heart and life during that difficult time. I pray that it will be useful to you and that God will give you much hope and strength through it.

This course is designed to be complementary to the Setting Captives Free Purity Boot Camp book. Purity Boot Camp is the book your spouse who is seeking freedom from sexual impurity will go through.

I knew a little of my husband's involvement with sexual impurity before we married, but I naively believed once we married, I could meet all his sexual needs so thoroughly that sexual immorality would no longer tempt him. I can see how ignorant I was. I was unaware of sin and its power, and I was prideful to think I could prevent my husband from sinning; only God can change a heart and keep any of us from falling into sin (Jude 1:24).

After we were married, I fell into a habit of rationalizing away any suspicions I had about my husband's involvement with sexual sin. I wanted to believe the best of him and, besides; I did not know how to deal with the problem. Eventually, the evidence and corresponding marital troubles became so glaring that I knew I had to deal with it, but I was hurt and afraid. I didn't understand why my husband was acting this way, and I didn't know what to do to make it stop.

We had recently started attending a church where the pastor was also a biblical counselor. So, I approached our pastor and shared my concerns; our pastor was reassuring and comforting but also firm in his direction. Our pastor told me I would need to speak with my husband about his sin lovingly. He taught me that to truly love someone, is to want to see them successful in their walk with Christ. So, if I truly loved Mike, I would need to approach him in love with the goal of restoring our relationship.

The problem was that I was afraid, and I did not want to tell my husband what I had discovered. I didn't even know how, but, thankfully, my pastor helped me. Mike initially responded positively to our loving reproof, but the months that followed were hard.

I hoped that once I approached Mike with the evidence of his sin, he would confess and ask for forgiveness, and then everything would be okay again. I just wanted us to leave the sin behind and get on with our lives, but that isn't how things work with sin. Mike repented of his sin of sexual impurity, but that did not mean that the temptations were gone. In fact, for a while, it seemed they grew even more intense!

It became immediately apparent to us that we needed to change our way of thinking and living to protect ourselves from the attacks of the devil.

Under our pastor's instruction, we learned how to unite in love and spiritual warfare. We did whatever we could to work together to overcome this struggle that nearly destroyed our marriage.

Mike and I sought ways to rebuild our relationship. It was not an easy road to travel but, now I can look back and rejoice at God's grace and mercy in bringing us through this fire so that our marriage might be founded on the gospel of grace. By God's grace and power, my husband is walking in purity, and we remain united in love and the gospel.

Friend, we would like to help you. Please share a little about the struggles you are facing and about your family life by answering the following questions.

Question 1: Please tell us how you found out that your spouse is involved with sexual impurity and what, if anything, you have done about it?

Question 2: Have you put your faith in Jesus? If so, it would be wonderful to hear a brief testimony of how you came to faith in Christ. Please share.

_____

_____

_____

_____

Question 3: Is your spouse a professing Christian?
- ☐ Yes
- ☐ No
- ☐ Unsure

Question 4: Do you and your spouse regularly attend a local church?
- ☐ Yes
- ☐ No
- ☐ I go alone

Question 5: If yes, tell us about your local church's involvement. Have they helped you? If yes, how?

_____

_____

_____

_____

Question 6: How long have you been married?
- ☐ not married yet
- ☐ married less than a year
- ☐ 1-5 years
- ☐ 5-10 years
- ☐ 10-15 years
- ☐ 15 to 20 years
- ☐ more than 20 years

Question 7: Are you living with your spouse?
- ☐ yes
- ☐ no

Question 8: Do you have children?
- ☐ yes
- ☐ no

Question 9: Please tell us more about your family and home life. Please describe your daily life. What are your biggest struggles currently?

_____

_____

_____

_____

Question 10: What are your feelings about everything that has happened so far?

_____

_____

_____

_____

As we move forward into the teaching aspect of this course, I pray that you will find the lessons helpful. If you are like me, you probably have a lot of questions, and I do hope to address all your concerns in the course material, but this will take time.

I know it is hard to be patient when you are feeling pressed and in pain, but there are no quick fixes or easy answers for the issues of life. There is, however, comfort, healing, and hope in Jesus, so I invite you to go through these next thirty lessons with me. God brought you to this course for a reason, and I don't want you to miss out on the joy He has for you in Jesus and the practical solution for addressing the issue of sexual impurity in your marriage.

Gospel Hope

Welcome to lesson 1 of the A United Front course. I am sorry for the circumstances that brought you here but eager to share some good news and to comfort you as you seek the Lord during this difficult time.

As you read in the introduction, sexual impurity assaulted my marriage, and it was terrible. My husband and I were both like the man beaten and left half-dead on the road to Jericho (Luke 10:30-37) - broken and in need of help.

Maybe you are here today, thinking, as I once did, that your marriage is a lost cause. You feel hopeless and weary. Well, come with me through these lessons and allow me to share with you the comfort and instruction that I received from Christ. What we will find together is that there is real life-sustaining and transforming hope in Jesus as well as practical instruction from God's Word.

Yes, God has brought me through many trials in my life, and I boldly testify that there is no hurt too deep that God cannot heal it, no obstacle too great that God cannot overcome it.

Out of love for us, God sent His Son Jesus to die on the cross to save us, heal our broken hearts, mend our lives, and restore our relationship with Him and with each other. He has not and will not abandon us in our time of need.

There is real hope for our spouse too. The Bible provides us with many examples of men and women who committed all manner of sin but then repented, were forgiven and restored - King David (2 Samuel 11, Psalm 51), the woman at the well (John 4), the woman caught in adultery (John 8), Peter who denied Christ, and Paul who persecuted the church, to name a few. Seeing how God transformed these lives gives us hope for our own situations.

Now, look with me to see the hope that God conveys in the following passage:

"Come, let us return to the LORD. He has torn us to pieces but he will heal us; he has injured us, but he will bind up our wounds. 2 After two days he will revive us; on the third day he will restore us, that we may live in his presence." Hosea 6:1-2 NIV

Question 1: Please read Hosea 6:1-2. How does this passage give us hope?
- ☐ It tells us that the injury and wounds are too deep, and that healing might not be possible.
- ☐ It shows that God Himself revives and restores us. It says that after the wounding, God will heal, revive and restore us.
- ☐ It tells us that if we work hard, we can have hope for our marriage.

Hosea is a minor prophet; his book is in the Old Testament portion of the Bible. If we were to read the whole book of Hosea, we would quickly see the similarities between our lives and Hosea's since his wife betrayed him through sexual immorality. It is heartbreaking to read his book, but he told his story with a purpose.

Hosea's tumultuous marriage was symbolic of the nation of Israel and their unfaithfulness to God. Israel had run after other gods (spiritual adultery) and broken their covenant with God which meant that they were now under a curse.

But God did not abandon them in their sin. We can see in Hosea 6:1-3 that God had a plan for dealing with sin and brokenness, and this same plan is what gives us hope for the restoration of our marriages too.

First, we can see that Hosea 6:1 acknowledges the devastation of sin. The words torn, injured, and wounded are so appropriate. It is how I felt in the face of my husband's betrayal. I had a broken heart, a wounded spirit, and an injured marriage.

Question 2: Can you relate to the words Hosea used—torn, injured and wounded? Please share how you feel about your situation.

_____

_____

_____

_____

Now notice the invitation given to those of us who have been torn, wounded and injured: *"Come, let us return to the Lord…"*

Oh, friend, receive this good word today. In your sorrow and pain, Jesus is calling to you. His arms are spread open wide, inviting you to run into them and feel His loving embrace. He sees your broken heart, your torn marriage; and He is ready to bind you up and bring you to a place of rest and healing.

Question 3: Do you desire to receive the healing that Jesus has for you? If yes, and you would like, use the space to pour out your heart to God and tell Him that you want the healing that He has for you.

_____

_____

_____

_____

It is essential to understand that this invitation from Jesus is for your spouse too. This course is about becoming A United Front with your spouse, and if possible, you want to come to Jesus with your spouse.

Question 4: Has your spouse indicated a desire to repent and return to the Lord with you? Please share.

_____

_____

_____

_____

When we come to the Lord, He will heal us and bind up our wounds, but how does He do this? Hosea 6:2 says, *"After two days He will revive us, on the third day He will restore us."* But how does He revive us and restore us?

In this passage, we can see an arrow pointing to God's plan for dealing with the sin and broken covenants throughout time - the gospel of Jesus Christ.

God sent Jesus, who bore the curse of the broken covenant (Gal. 3:13). He took the wrath of God, was wounded and then died on the cross but *"was raised on the third day in accordance with the Scriptures"* (1 Cor. 15:4). Jesus laid down his life for us, His bride, the church (Eph. 5:25), and we as believers were *"in Him"* (Romans 6:3-9)! On the cross, His body was torn to shreds, but the amazing truth is that by His wounds, we are healed (Isaiah 53, I Peter 2:24)!

Sin destroys, but God restores. It is at the cross of Christ that we find healing for our wounds. We will see this increasingly as we continue in our study together.

We cannot fix the damage that sexual impurity inflicts, only God can do this, and He did it by sending Jesus to receive the intentional suffering of the cross. Jesus took on Himself all our sorrow and the sin of sexual impurity so that He might "bind up" of our wounds and provide healing to our hearts, lives, and marriages.

On the cross, Jesus was *"binding up our wounds"* even as He received His own deep wounds. Oh, friend, no matter how ugly sin is, it cannot quench God's redeeming love. Where sin abounds, God's grace abounds even more (Romans 5:20)!

As I came to understand these truths, I felt my heart beginning to mend. The more I experienced the love of Christ from the cross (1 John 4:10 NIV), the greater the healing that came to my heart and my marriage. All the anger, fear, bitterness, and anxiety that sexual impurity brought to my mind, Jesus cast out with His great, sacrificial, life-saving love (1 John 4:18).

> **Question 5:** As you look at the cross and see Jesus suffering in your place to heal you, what does it do for your heart?

_____

_____

_____

_____

Hosea 6:2 says that God will revive and restore you which points forward to the fact that you were counted *"in Christ"* when He died, and when He rose from the dead. The same power that raised Jesus from the dead is active in you if you are a believer (Romans 6:4, 8:11; Ephesians 1:19-20).

Yes, there is real hope for you in Jesus for, not only did He suffer to bind up your wounds, but He also has resurrection power that can change everything. Maybe you feel like your marriage is dying or already dead, but just as Jesus was raised from the dead, even so, Jesus raises dead marriages! There is hope for you and your spouse in Christ!

We can also learn from this passage that the healing that God provides might take time. *"After two days, He will revive us; on the third day, He will restore us"* (Hosea 6:2). Healing is not always instantaneous as there may be time between being *"torn to shreds"* (Hosea 6:1) and being *"restored"* (Hosea 6:2). This passage tells you that you can have hope in God to heal, restore, and provide strength in His time.

As my husband was coming out of impurity, life for us was like a roller coaster. He was up one day and down the next. He would be demanding one day and kind and loving the next. For a long time, I rode these ups and downs with him—it was emotionally exhausting!

If you're experiencing this instability too, I want to share with you how I found hope and faith to persevere, and how you can also. It goes right along with our subject of today. Stability comes from finding genuine hope in God and the gospel.

Consider the following passage of Scripture from the book of Hebrews. It helps to know that the book of Hebrews was written to Jewish Christians who lived in a time of opposition and persecution. They were attacked from within and without. They needed the same kind of hope that we need.

> *God did this so that, by two unchangeable things in which it is impossible for God to lie, we who have fled to take hold of the hope offered to us may be greatly encouraged. 19 We have this hope as an anchor for the soul, firm and secure. It enters the inner sanctuary behind the curtain, Hebrews 6:18-19 NIV*

I love these verses! For those of us who've been lied to time and time again, it is so comforting to know that *"it is impossible for God to lie."* We can trust Him and run to Him to take hold of the hope offered to us in the gospel of Jesus Christ.

Question 6: According to Hebrews 6:19, what is it that will "anchor" our souls?
- ☐ Our souls will be anchored when our husbands stop sinning.
- ☐ Our souls will be anchored when God fixes our marriage.
- ☐ Our souls are anchored in steadfast gospel hope, and we can take hold of it now.

Oh, friend, if you are hurting and feeling tossed back and forth like a ship without an anchor, let me share with you the anchor I found that held me safely through this storm. My anchor is Jesus, and, specifically, what He accomplished for me on the cross and in His resurrection. I learned how to depend on Him and trust in Him so that regardless of my circumstances, I am safe in Him. This hope I have in my Lord Jesus Christ is an anchor for my soul, and it can be for you, too.

Question 7: This lesson was on having hope in the gospel. Why is it important for you to hope in the gospel of Jesus Christ when facing the trial of sexual impurity in your marriage?

_____

_____

_____

_____

Pathway to Healing

*W*elcome back to the A United Front course. As you begin today, know that God loves you, and I am praying for you.

When first dealing with the issue of sexual impurity in my marriage, my prayers were mostly comprised of me begging God to make my husband stop his sexual sinning, repent, and be faithful to me. But over time, I discovered that my way of doing things was not like God's at all.

It was hard to have hope when it seemed that nothing was getting better until I realized that God was addressing heart issues that were beyond my immediate understanding. Now, looking back, I can see that God was always working just not in ways that I expected.

Yesterday, we spoke of having hope in the gospel of Jesus Christ. We saw that at the cross, Jesus not only forgives our sins, but He also heals our wounds and mends our broken hearts. We read, *"After two days he will revive us; on the third day he will restore us" (Hosea 6:1-2).*

There is a corresponding passage found in 1 Peter that reads, *"after you have suffered a little while, the God of all grace, who has called you to his eternal glory in Christ, will himself restore, confirm, strengthen, and establish you" (1 Peter 5:10).*

Question 1: According to 1 Peter 5:10, because of the gospel of Jesus Christ, what will happen to you? Please fill in the blanks: "After you have suffered a little while, the God of all grace...will Himself _____, _____, _____ and _____ you."

Today, I want to talk with you about the pathway to this restoration; the pathway to healing and to being strengthened by God. But be prepared, this pathway might not be what you expect.

To see this pathway to healing, let's read more from 1 Peter 5:

"6 Humble yourselves, therefore, under the mighty hand of God so that at the proper time he may exalt you, 7 casting all your anxieties on him, because he cares for you. 8 Be sober-minded; be watchful. Your adversary the devil prowls around like a roaring lion, seeking someone to devour. 9 Resist him, firm in your faith, knowing that the same kinds of suffering are being experienced by your brotherhood throughout the world. 10 And after you have suffered a little while, the God of all grace, who has called you to his eternal glory in Christ, will himself restore, confirm, strengthen, and establish you." 1 Peter 5:6–10

Question 2: According to 1 Peter 5:6, what is the first thing we should do in order to draw near to God and lay hold of the healing and restoration He has for us?
- ☐ Cast our cares on Jesus.
- ☐ Humble ourselves.
- ☐ Be watchful.

The first step on our pathway to healing is humility. We must humble ourselves and submit to God in all things. We must look beyond the surface of our spouse's sin and see that God is working, but this is easier said than done.

My first thought, when reading "humble yourselves," was "That's right! My husband needs to humble himself and repent of his sins right now!" But eventually, I realized that I too needed to humble myself before God and repent of my sins. I wanted to draw near to God, but my victim mentality was keeping me from experiencing the grace of God and robbing me of the joy of my salvation.

Many want to treat those who struggle with sexual impurity like the Pharisees treated the woman caught in adultery (John 8:1-11). They publicly shamed her and wanted to stone her, but Jesus showed us that this is a wrong and ineffective approach. We cannot shame people into repentance. As Jesus quietly wrote on the sand that day, the accusers were humbled! And as they crept away from Jesus, they left the woman with the only One (Jesus) who had a right to condemn her but would not. Instead, Jesus forgave her sin and told her to go and sin no more (John 8:11).

Jesus is the incarnation of humility and showed us by example, how to walk the road of humility. Philippians 2 tells us, *"In your relationships with one another, have the same mindset as Christ Jesus: Who, being in very nature God, did not consider equality with God something to be used to his own advantage; rather, he made himself nothing by taking the very nature of a servant, being made in human likeness. And being found in appearance as a man, he humbled himself by becoming obedient to death—even death on a cross!" Philippians 2:5-8 (NIV)*

Our Jesus (the Lord of Glory) humbled Himself, took our sins upon Himself, died and rose again so that we might have eternal life through Him. And God's Word tells us to, *"Have the same mindset."*

We are not without sin; so, we should not cast stones, but rather walk with Jesus in humility. When we do, we draw near to God and experience the healing that Jesus has purchased for us on the cross.

Question 3: According to 1 Peter 5:6, after we humble ourselves, what does God do?
- ☐ God hurts those who hurt us.
- ☐ At the proper time, God exalts us.
- ☐ God gives us whatever we want.

Question 4: When it comes to desiring restoration, strengthening by God and healing, why it is important to embrace humility?

_____

_____

_____

_____

Yes, when we humble ourselves and seek the Lord, He exalts us at the proper time. I saw this happen in my marriage. As long as I was proud, angry, and accusing, my husband was prickly, defensive, and accusatory; but when I humbled myself before God and my husband something began to change. My husband began to see that we were on the same side and working to help each other. We started to become a united front against the devil. God, in His amazing way, began to lift us both up as He taught us how to focus on Jesus and the gospel.

> **Question 5:** When desiring healing and restoration, what is the second thing we are called to do? Please fill in the blank. 1 Peter 5:7, "casting all your _____ on him, because he _____ for you."

When I first discovered my husband's sin, I was frightened and confused. My mind was consumed with how to cope with the present, and I had serious concerns about the future. I was anxious about where my husband was and what he was doing. I fretted when we were physically intimate wondering if he was thinking about another person. I worried about our children and how they would be affected. It was horrible!

But Jesus taught me to bring my fears to Him. It took a lot of practice. Sometimes I would cast my cares on Christ only to reel them right back to myself; but in time, I learned to leave my anxieties with Jesus. May God enable you to do this too.

> **Question 6:** Do you have any anxieties that you need to cast on Jesus today? Please write them out here, and we will pray with you:

> _____

> _____

> _____

> _____

The next step of our path to restoration and healing is 1 Peter 5:8-9a, *"Be sober-minded; be watchful. Your adversary the devil prowls around like a roaring lion, seeking someone to devour. Resist him..."*

Dear friend, the devil wants to destroy Christian marriages. He wants to tear our families apart as a lion tears apart his prey, and he will use whatever means he can. You might be hurting deeply from your spouse's betrayal, but it is important to remember that pain can distort our thinking. We must resist the desire to respond to our spouses in a reactionary and ordinary way, and instead, look to Christ and follow His lead.

God calls us to be "sober-minded." We should not be intoxicated or medicated in a way that would prevent us from having clear and godly thinking. It is natural to want to escape our pain and numb it with food, alcohol, or medications; but these responses will only make our situation worse.

Additionally, we must take this issue of fighting for our marriages seriously. We are in a battle against dark forces in dark places (Ephesians 6:12), but we do not face the darkness alone. We stand in Jesus, the Light that overcomes!

> **Question 7:** Are you being sober-minded? Please explain the nature of any struggles that you are having.
>
> _____
>
> _____
>
> _____
>
> _____

You are not alone, friend! This is contrary to what most of us feel. The sin of sexual impurity lends itself to isolation, and Satan would like nothing more than to convince us that we are the only ones struggling with these difficult issues.

The reality is that this is a common struggle. Thousands of people from around the world and from all walks of life come to Setting Captives Free every day to find help to break free from habitual sin.

One of our family doctors once said to us, "Your problem is unique and difficult, but only to you. I see this same problem multiple times a day." And so, it is with us, friend; our problems loom large and frighten us, but only from our point of view. Our Great Physician is the Solution for us all.

Now we come to the joyful part of our path, 1 Peter 5:10, *"And after you have suffered a little while, the God of all grace, who has called you to his eternal glory in Christ, will himself restore, confirm, strengthen, and establish you..."*

Oh, dear friend, God HIMSELF will restore you, confirm you, strengthen you and put your feet in a stable place once more. I understand that right now, you may not know how God will do this, but God promised to do it, and He cannot lie. If we entrust ourselves to God and look to the cross of Christ where His love is poured out then *"after you have suffered a little while,"* you will experience the restoration and healing you want and need.

Do you see how 1 Peter 5:6-10 is a practical application of the gospel of Jesus Christ? In the gospel, Jesus humbled Himself unto death, even death on the cross. Then, on the third day, He rose from the dead, was restored, confirmed, strengthened, and established.

Likewise, as you humble yourself to learn the gospel way of responding to your husband, as you humble yourself to become a partner with your husband against impurity, your healing and restoration will come.

Friend, Christ humbled Himself and walked obediently to death on a cross to be our atoning sacrifice, but three days later He arose from the grave victorious and was exalted to the right hand of the Father! There is a resurrection! Your days might be dark right now but hold on for the restoration that is coming.

Question 8: What do you want to remember about this lesson? What are your final thoughts?

Healing in Jesus

*W*elcome back to your course. I hope you are finding your time here beneficial.

So far, we've talked about how our hope and healing flow from the gospel of Jesus Christ. We follow Christ in humility, we suffer for a little while, and at the proper time, God lifts us, restores and strengthens us.

In this lesson, we will talk about what to do with all our feelings of pain while we are waiting on the Lord for our healing and the restoration of our marriage and about how to receive the healing God has for us.

Sexual sin is uniquely hurtful and stirs up distressing thoughts in our minds because it touches us at the most intimate part of our lives. When I discovered my husband's sexual impurity, it was as if someone had taken a knife and plunged it into my heart and then poured fear, anger, dread, and immense sorrow into the open wound. I felt rejected; my spirit was crushed. I wondered, "Why is God letting my husband do these wicked things? What did I do to deserve this? How can a loving God allow this to happen?" It was a very dark time in my life.

Question 1: Are there any thoughts or feelings troubling your heart and mind today? Please share.

_____

_____

_____

_____

As we saw in previous lessons, God understands what it is to have an unfaithful spouse. God made a covenant with His people, Israel, and they broke it in every way possible. For this reason, many of the books in the Old Testament talk about Israel's unfaithfulness and God's response to it.

The book of Isaiah is no exception, but like Hosea, Isaiah also sheds light on God's plan of hope and restoration for His people. And it is in his book that we find the biblical foundation for our lesson today.

Please look with me at Isaiah 53:2-5 understanding that this passage, according to Acts 8:35, is speaking about Jesus Christ.

> "He grew up before him like a tender shoot, and like a root out of dry ground. He had no beauty or majesty to attract us to him, nothing in his appearance that we should desire him. 3 He was despised and rejected by mankind, a man of suffering, and familiar with pain. Like one from whom people hide their faces he was despised, and we held him in low esteem. Surely, he took up our pain and bore our suffering, yet we considered him punished by God, stricken by him, and afflicted. But he was pierced for our transgressions, he was crushed for our iniquities; the punishment that brought us peace was on him, and by his wounds, we are healed."

Question 2: As you read the description of Jesus in Isaiah 53, what stood out to you? Share your thoughts.

_____

_____

_____

_____

Seven hundred years before Jesus was born, Isaiah wrote about Jesus and the sufferings Jesus would endure to save us, His people. Thousands of years later, in my time of difficulty, I read the description of Jesus in verses 2-3 and related to it so much. Jesus was rejected by His own. Me too. Others were more attractive and desirable than He was (verse 2). I felt that way too. He was a man of sorrows (verse 3). I was a woman of sorrow. As I read, I felt like Jesus and I were sharing the same experience, and this made me feel closer to Him because of it. Then as I kept reading, I understood why. Jesus knew my sorrow because He had already carried it before me.

> **Question 3:** According to Isaiah 53:4 NIV, what did Jesus carry when He went to the cross? *"Surely he took up our _____ and bore our _____;"* Isaiah 53:4

At one point, I thought that if my husband could just feel my pain, if only he could understand how his sin hurt me, then he'd stop doing it. So, I tried to make him understand. I would cry and try to explain the depth of hurt I felt.

However, this emptying of my pain on to my husband only made things worse. My efforts to make my husband feel my pain made him feel so guilty and ashamed that he would end up falling back into sin, trying to escape the pain of his failures.

Pouring out our sorrows and pain to our spouse does not bring healing to our hearts or repentance to their lives. Instead, we must come to the One who has carried our griefs and sorrows.

As Jesus climbed the hill of Calvary to His death, He was carrying your sorrow and mine. He was bearing the weight of all the sin that had been and would be committed, and all the suffering and grief that comes with it, in his heart, body, and mind. Every step was anguish. Every breath was arduous; his wounds were excruciating. So, when we come to Him and pour out our pain, He not only hears, but He also understands like no one else ever will.

In Psalm 62:8, we are encouraged to pour out our hearts to God because He is our refuge. Friend, this is so true. You can safely pour out your heart to God. He is a safe Refuge for you now and always. He carried all your pain and sorrow and grief, all the wounds and heartache you feel, all the sin and suffering of the world.

Question 4: Take a moment to pour out your heart to God. Release to Him your pain, fear, frustration, whatever you are feeling. We will unite in prayer with you.

_____

_____

_____

_____

It is often true that people who have been where we are know how to speak words of help to us, better than others who have not experienced what we are going through.

If you are suffering and in anguish, today, remember that Jesus knows your sorrow intimately because He carried it up the hill of Golgotha and died with it in his heart. And because Jesus knows your sadness and grief, He can speak healing to it in the way that you need; it might not be in a way that you expect though. When Jesus speaks healing, He does not use mere words. No, Jesus steps into our need and meets it fully with His love in action.

Question 5: According to Isaiah 53:5, by what are we healed?
- ☐ The Holy Spirit heals us.
- ☐ Prayer heals us.
- ☐ The wounds of Jesus heal us.

Jesus willingly subjected Himself to the pain and humiliation of our sorrow, sin, and shame because He was able to overcome it where we never could. His wounds were intentional and purposeful. They achieved for us the forgiveness of our sins, peace with God and healing for our wounded hearts and relationships.

True healing for our wounded souls comes through identification with Christ on His cross. We cannot look to our spouse or others for healing because they were not designed to provide it; they are also wounded people. We cannot look to ourselves for healing because the wound is too great. We must look to Christ and His wounds because this is the Solution that God has provided.

As we look to Christ and His wounds for healing, what we see is His overwhelming love, and we are comforted by it! In Psalm 119:76, the psalmist cries, "*Let your steadfast love comfort me…*" And in 1 John 3:16 we learn that Christ's work on the cross for us is the very definition of love: "*This is how we know what love is: Jesus Christ laid down his life for us*" *1 John 3:16a NIV*

"*This is love: not that we loved God, but that he loved us and sent his Son as an atoning sacrifice for our sins.*" *1 John 4:10 NIV*

Oh, friend, looking to the cross is where we will receive our healing. If you look at the cross right now, you will see God's eternal love for you. There Jesus hangs between heaven and earth, between God and man, being rejected by both! Do you see His heartfelt love for you there?

> *John 13:1 (NIV) It was just before the Passover Festival. Jesus knew that the hour had come for him to leave this world and go to the Father. Having **loved** his own who were in the world, he **loved them to the end.***

This is a love that would rather die for you than live without you, love that would hang in darkness on a criminal's cross for you. Let this love begin to comfort you and start to heal your wounded heart.

Jesus told His disciples, "*In this world, you will have trouble. But take heart! I have overcome the world.*" This is true for us as well. In this life, we will sin and be sinned against, but through His death on the cross, Jesus made atonement for both. At the cross, we receive forgiveness for our sins and healing for our souls because Jesus has taken on our sins and our sorrows and overcome!

Question 6: Are you looking to Christ and His cross for healing today?
- ☐ Yes
- ☐ No
- ☐ I have questions about this topic.

I hope that you are looking to Christ and His wounds for your healing, but if you are struggling with it, I understand. My healing was not instantaneous either.

In Genesis 32, we read the biblical account of a man named Jacob who was facing his own time of "great fear and distress" (Genesis 32:7). In his time of need, Jacob cries out to God, *"Save me, I pray..."* And that very night, God in the form of a man (Jesus) comes to Jacob, and they wrestle all night long. At daybreak, Jacob says, *"I will not let you go unless you bless me."* (Genesis 32:26) And God does bless Jacob.

I urge you to come to Jesus, look to His death on the cross, see His love, and hold on to Him until you are healed and comforted. God is faithful; He will do it (1 Thessalonians 5:24).

Today, my heart today is mended and full of the love of Jesus. God has healed my marriage and made it better than it was before the wounding. My husband is strong in the Lord and walking in purity. And we are one couple out of millions that God has healed and restored.

Your faith is well placed in Christ. Trust Him. He is our Savior and Healer.

Question 7: What are your final thoughts about today's lesson?

_____

_____

_____

_____

How to be a Helper

Welcome back, friend. Today, we are going to move forward in the love of God, in humility, and by the power of the gospel towards becoming a united front with our spouses against the devil and his schemes.

To begin, let's consider where the concept of "A United Front" finds its origin. The husband and wife team was God's design from the beginning; we can see this in *Genesis 2:18 (NIV), The Lord God said, "It is not good for the man to be alone. I will make a helper suitable for him."* God declared that it wasn't good for the man to be alone, so God created the woman to be his helper. This truth is reiterated in 1 Corinthians 11:9, which tells us that woman was created for man.

You might be thinking, "I know this already, but we are talking about sin. My husband needs to own his sin and deal with it." It is true, Romans 14:12 teaches that each of us will give a personal account before God.

But it is also true that when we married, we became one with our spouse and this oneness makes us responsible before God to help our spouse in all things, including overcoming sin struggles (Genesis 2:24, Ephesians 5:31).

> **Question 1:** Please fill in the blank: "The Lord God said, "It is not good for the man to be _____. I will make a _____ suitable for him."

Now that we understand we can and should help our spouse overcome their sin struggles, let's talk about ways we can help.

The first and most important way that we can help our spouse is for us to be gospel-centered people.

Hebrews 12:1-3 will explain; please read it with me:

Therefore, since we are surrounded by so great a cloud of witnesses, let us also lay aside every weight, and sin which clings so closely, and let us run with endurance the race that is set before us, 2 looking to Jesus, the founder and perfecter of our faith, who for the joy that was set before him endured the cross, despising the shame, and is seated at the right hand of the throne of God. 3 Consider him who endured from sinners such hostility against himself, so that you may not grow weary or fainthearted. (Hebrews 12:1-3, ESV)

Question 2: According to Hebrews 12:2, to whom should we look as we run "the race" set before us?
- ☐ Our pastor.
- ☐ Jesus.
- ☐ Our friends.

We look to Jesus. We should not look to our parents, siblings, or friends to save us, though certainly if these individuals live their lives in line with the gospel, they will encourage our hearts and may be useful in our lives (Hebrews 10:24). But ultimately, we cannot look to any human to sustain us as we stand against the devil and learn how to help our husbands. Such a fight needs supernatural power which can only come from our precious Savior Jesus.

Question 3: According to Hebrews 12:3, what about Jesus should we "consider" so that we do not grow weary and lose heart?
- ☐ His good life and example.
- ☐ His teaching and miracles.
- ☐ His death on the cross.

Oh, friend, Jesus endured a horrible and agonizing death on the cross so that we might be forgiven of our sins and filled with His Spirit. No agony we ever face in this life is ever going to come close to what Jesus endured. No battle we fight will ever be near to the one Jesus encountered. He became sin for you and drank the full cup of God's wrath for you, thus enabling you to be free of punishment.

This is good news for us because as we consider Christ and all that He has done on our behalf, we are filled with hope. Not only can we find healing and forgiveness for ourselves at the cross, but our spouses can be forgiven and restored as well.

Focusing on the cross, seeing Jesus' sacrificial love, experiencing the forgiveness He purchased for you and the atonement He made for you will keep you from growing weary or fainthearted along the way.

> **Question 4:** What does focusing on the cross of Jesus do for your heart and mind? Please share your thoughts.

_____

_____

_____

_____

The road we walk is difficult; we need the hope, courage, and joy of the gospel for the journey ahead. As we move forward in these lessons, I will encourage you to do some difficult things, and in your own strength, you will not be able to do what needs to be done. But God is faithful, and He can work in and through you (Philippians 2:13; 1 Thessalonians 5:24).

Let us now consider the biblical instruction given to us regarding how to respond to the sexual sin of our spouse. Read with me Matthew 18:15-17:

> *"If your brother sins against you, go and tell him his fault, between you and him alone. If he listens to you, you have gained your brother. But if he does not listen, take one or two others along with you, that every charge may be established by the evidence of two or three witnesses. If he refuses to listen to them, tell it to the church. Matthew 18: 15-17 (ESV)*

Question 5: According to Matthew 18:15, what did Jesus say we should do when our Christian spouse sins against us? And what is the goal of doing this?

- ☐ Call the pastor so that he can discipline your spouse
- ☐ Talk to your spouse and invite them to repent so your relationship can be restored.
- ☐ Throw your spouse out so they see the error of their ways.

The first instruction given is to go to our spouse privately and talk with them face to face. We do not want to talk to others about our husband's sin at this point. This is a very important conversation, and it should be approached with care. None of us enjoys seeing our own sin. You will want to approach your spouse with gentleness and grace just as you would want someone to approach you about your own sin struggles.

Proverbs 15:4 NCV tells us, *"As a tree gives fruit, healing words give life"* and we want to have healing and hopeful words for our spouse when we approach them about their sexual sin.

To get these healing words, we must come to the cross of Christ and ask God to help us. Ask Him to reveal to you any personal sins for which you should seek forgiveness (Matthew 7: 1-5) and ask Him for grace to be kind no matter how your spouse responds (Ephesians 4:32). Also, pray that God would grant repentance to your spouse.

Before talking with your spouse, I recommend writing out what you want to say so that you can be clear and focused; this will also allow you to stay purposeful in your conversation and help you to avoid angry and bitter words. I find it helpful to reverse the roles and imagine what I would want to hear if I were the one being confronted with my sin issue. Remember that gospel words are the most healing words because they give the hope of forgiveness and restoration.

Finally, be sure to choose your timing carefully. It's better not to have this conversation when you are busy or exhausted. Make sure that you do all you can to put your spouse at ease, and then in love, talk with them plainly and clearly about your concerns.

Here is a sample conversation to consider:

Honey, I need to talk to you for a few minutes. Is this a good time? Okay. First, I want to say that I love and appreciate you and that's why I'm coming to you now with a concern that I have.

I saw some pornographic websites in our computer history. We both know that sexually immoral material like that is not good for us.

I'm not angry; I'm a sinner too. Which is why I am so glad that Jesus died on the cross for us to remove the sin and shame of our sins.

I know it is hard to avoid pornography because it seems like it is everywhere, so I want to do all I can to help you avoid it. What can I do to help?

Question 6: Please write out what you would say to your spouse when you speak with them about their sin issue:

_____

_____

_____

_____

If your husband hears you and accepts your offer of help, then you have won your spouse. Rejoice. You will want to continue working together to prevent future falls and to foster healing in your marriage; we will cover these things in future lessons.

But what if your husband doesn't respond well? This is a possibility and is why Jesus addressed it. Let's look at Matthew 18:16 again, *"But if he does not listen, take one or two others along with you..." (Matthew 18:16a)*

If your spouse doesn't respond well to your first approach, then you need to involve one or two other people. This can be a hard thing to do, which is why you need to be careful in choosing the others that you involve.

Ideally, you will want to choose Christians that your spouse respects to assist you—this could be a pastor, teacher, biblical counselor, a Christian couple. Choose whomever you believe will have the most positive impact on your situation. It will help if you plan the interaction ahead of time so that the godly man can present a plan of repentance and restoration and offer his assistance in accountability.

This was the winning factor in my situation; when our pastor offered my husband love and godly help, my husband rejoiced and accepted with joy because he wanted to repent, he just didn't know how to do it.

But should your spouse refuse to listen to you and the others that have come alongside you, Christ gives the following instruction:

"If he refuses to listen to them, tell it to the church..." (Matthew 18:17)

If our spouse refuses to listen to us or the others we bring, then we must go to our church leadership for their guidance and assistance. This is not meant to be punitive but rather restorative. Church discipline is designed to be an act of God's mercy and love, and it can be effective, as in the case of the man who was restored out of a life of sexual sin back to the Corinthian church in 2 Corinthians 2:7-11.

Question 7: Have you implemented any of these biblical principles yet? Please share.

_____

_____

_____

_____

Friend, I hope that you have been encouraged by the clear instruction that God has given regarding how to approach your sinning spouse. I know implementing these truths can be challenging, but as you fix your eyes on Jesus and follow Him, He will enable you to move forward in His love.

Forgiveness
Our Sin Debt has been Paid by Jesus

*I*n the previous lesson, we learned about the importance of being gospel-centered people. It is the good news of Christ's finished work on the cross and His resurrection that can empower us to move forward in love and reconciliation *without growing weary*. It is the gospel that gives us the grace to say "no" to responding to our spouse's sin struggle in an ungodly way and "yes" to responding with Jesus' love.

We also studied Jesus' counsel from Matthew 18 regarding how to deal with a sinning brother or sister in Christ. We first need to talk with our spouse, and if they hear us, then we forgive them and work toward growing in grace together.

But if our spouse does not listen, then we are to involve one or two other Christians who will work with us to encourage our spouse toward repentance. If our spouse still does not listen, then we are to go to our church leaders who will help us take the matter to the church. The church will encourage our spouse toward repentance, unite with us in prayer for the restoration of our marriage, and help us to respond to our situation in a gospel-focused way so that God will be glorified through it all.

Today, we will continue sitting at the feet of Jesus in Matthew 18, and we'll learn what He has to teach us about forgiveness and the reason we give it. Look with me now at Matthew 18:21-22:

> *"Then Peter came up and said to him, "Lord, how often will my brother sin against me, and I forgive him? As many as seven times?" Jesus said to him, "I do not say to you seven times, but seventy-seven times."*

In light of Jesus' instruction on how to respond to a brother or sister who sins against us, Peter's question is logical. Basically, Peter says to Jesus what all the disciples are thinking, "I understand I should forgive my brother, but how many times must I forgive?" And notice how Peter even suggests a number that he thinks is generous—seven.

By nature, we are all like Peter; we want to set limits on forgiveness that seem reasonable to us. We fear being taken advantage of, being seen as foolish, or that forgiveness will cause the offender to think what he did is okay. But, as we will see in our lesson today, this way of thinking flows from a wrong perspective and understanding.

> **Question 1:** How many times does Jesus tell Peter that we should forgive those who sin against us? Fill in the blank. "Lord, _____ _____ will my brother sin against me, and I forgive him? As many as seven times?" Jesus said to him, "I do not say to you seven times, but _____-_____ times."

Now to be clear, Christ is not saying that we forgive a specific number of times, and then we are done. He is teaching that *forgiveness is to be given as often as necessary.*

> **Question 2:** How are you doing with forgiving your spouse for their sins against you? Please share.

Because Jesus knows us and our weaknesses (Hebrews 4:15), He uses a parable to give us the eternal outlook we need to do this repeated forgiving. Let's read the story:

"Therefore, the kingdom of heaven may be compared to a king who wished to settle accounts with his servants. When he began to settle, one was brought to him who owed him ten thousand talents. And since he could not pay, his master ordered him to be sold, with his wife and children and all that he had, and payment to be made. So, the servant fell on his knees, imploring him, 'Have patience with me, and I will pay you everything.' And out of pity for him, the master of that servant released him and forgave him the debt." Matthew 18:23-27

A parable is a story that teaches a moral or in our case, the principle of biblical forgiveness. In this parable, we see that a King had a servant who owed a great debt. The Greek word that Jesus used to describe the great debt this servant owed is *mýrioi,* which means an indefinitely large number, an amount too large to count.

This servant owed a massive debt, but he did not have the means to repay. Accordingly, the king, as was the custom at the time, commanded that the indebted servant be sold, along with his wife and children, into slavery and that all his possessions be sold to recoup some of the loss.

But then something happens that changes everything. The servant falls on his knees and begs for mercy! Amazingly, the king has pity, releases the servant, and forgives the debt. Notice the king does not agree to the servant's foolish request to have patience and give his servant more time to repay the debt. The king knows it is not possible for the servant to repay such a massive debt, so in an act of nobility and grace, the king forgives the unpayable debt. The servant walks out of the palace, debt-free, by a miracle of mercy.

Question 3: Each person in this parable is not a real person but a symbolic person. Who does the king in the story represent?
- ☐ God
- ☐ The Government
- ☐ The Church

Question 4: Who does the servant with the great debt represent?
- ☐ The Pharisees
- ☐ Jesus
- ☐ Me

This first part of the parable is a picture of God and us. We have all sinned (Romans 3:23); we come before God with an enormous debt of sin which we cannot repay. We deserve death and hell, but we cry out for mercy. And even though we might be willing to "work" off our debt, God knows this is not possible. This is why God sent Jesus to die on the cross.

On the cross, Jesus paid off our massive sin debt for us. *"He saved us, not because of works done by us in righteousness, but according to his own mercy, by the washing of regeneration and renewal of the Holy Spirit, whom he poured out on us richly through Jesus Christ our Savior..." Titus 3:5-6*

It is by Jesus' work on the cross that we are saved. The idea that our good works could ever cancel out even some of our sins is a lie of the devil. Our only hope is that we obtain mercy from God and have our debt of sin forgiven through the atoning blood of the Lord Jesus Christ.

Question 5: How do you know you have had your sin debt forgiven by King Jesus?

Let's continue with the story now and see how this servant responds to this amazing gift he has received:

But when that same servant went out, he found one of his fellow servants who owed him a hundred denarii and seizing him, he began to choke him, saying, 'Pay what you owe.' 29 So his fellow servant fell down and pleaded with him, 'Have patience with me, and I will pay you.' 30 He refused and went and put him in prison until he should pay the debt. Matthew 18:28-30

Did you notice how the servant with the small debt makes the same request of his fellow servant that the servant with the great debt made to the king? Were you shocked when the first servant refused to forgive the little debt and had his fellow servant put in prison?

When we sin against one another, we are essentially incurring a debt. This second servant, who owes the small debt, represents our brother or sister in Christ who has sinned against us.

Your spouse's sin of sexual impurity is a sin debt, but Jesus calls you to see it for what it is in light of His cross. Your sins and your spouse's sin debt has been paid for by Jesus. He paid the debt with His own blood. He calls you to live in His abundant grace and forgiveness and to forgive your spouse their sin debt as He has forgiven you.

This is difficult to read, isn't it? We love the forgiveness we receive from Christ, but when someone sins against us, our flesh gets angry or fearful and does not want to forgive. We might even want to act like this first servant and lash out to hurt our offender. But as we read on, we'll discover that this type of behavior is contrary to the Kingdom of Heaven.

As you read this next section, notice two things: how the fellow servants feel when they see one servant refusing to show mercy to another and how the king responds when he gets word of what has happened.

When his fellow servants saw what had taken place, they were greatly distressed, and they went and reported to their master all that had taken place. Then his master summoned him and said to him, 'You wicked servant! I forgave you all that debt because you pleaded with me. And should not you have had mercy on your fellow servant, as I had mercy on you?' And in anger, his master delivered him to the jailers until he should pay all his debt. So also, my heavenly Father will do to every one of you if you do not forgive your brother from your heart." Matthew 18: 31-35

Oh, friend, when we refuse to forgive those who sin against us, we distress the body of Christ and invite the discipline of God (Hebrews 12:5-8).

In short, Jesus has taught us through this parable that our massive sin debt has been forgiven and if we refuse to forgive from our hearts we are sinning. We have been forgiven an enormous debt—a lifetime of sin—it is right that we forgive others their small (in comparison) sins against us.

> **Question 6:** Why is it important to know that our own sin debt is forgiven when it comes to dealing with the sin of our spouse?

If you are struggling with forgiveness today, I urge you to come to Christ with your concerns. Sit at the foot of His cross and consider His wounds that plead for you. Receive His grace and love that He pours out along with His blood for you and be comforted by Him so that out of the abundance of mercy you receive from Him, you will be able to extend forgiveness to your spouse.

In the next lesson, we will be studying more about what biblical forgiveness is and what it isn't. Until then, may the mercy, peace and love of Jesus be yours in abundance.

LESSON 6:

Forgiven Forgivers

Welcome back, friend! As promised, we will continue our discussion of forgiveness today. I pray that you will find it helpful.

Yesterday, we studied the parable of the unforgiving servant. We learned that Jesus paid off our massive sin debt when He died on the cross. In light of what He has done for us, God expects us to show mercy to others and forgive them from our hearts as often as needed. And if we withhold forgiveness from our brothers or sisters in Christ, then we sin and invite the discipline of God (Hebrews 12:5-8).

It is clear that forgiveness is essential to God and His people, but questions frequently arise beyond how often we forgive. Questions such as:

- What does it mean to forgive?
- If I forgive, does that mean I'm okay with the sin?
- Does God expect me to forget the sin?
- Will my forgiveness mean there are no consequences?
- Do I forgive someone who is not repentant?

Let's explore the Scriptures together to find the answers we need.

First, let's establish what Biblical forgiveness is so that we might understand both what we have received from God through the death of His Son, and what we are giving to others when we grant forgiveness.

In the Bible, the Greek word translated as forgiveness means "to release, to pardon, to let go." The implication is that the forgiver releases the right to demand payment for a debt.

When Jesus died on the cross and made atonement for us, He purchased the complete forgiveness of our sins (1 John 2:2). Our sin debt has been canceled because Jesus paid it all! When Jesus cried out from the cross, *"It is finished!"* He was declaring publicly that our sin debt had been paid!

In Christ we have been shown mercy (Ephesians 2:4-10); and this is tremendously good news! Because of Christ's shed blood, there is total forgiveness of our sins (past, present, and future). Because we are covered by the blood of Christ, we enjoy a relationship with God and are able to draw near to Him (Hebrews 10:20). God chooses to not remember our sins (Hebrews 8:12). He does not hold our sins against us or treat us according to our sins (Psalm 103:10-12).

> **Question 1:** How does the forgiveness you have received from God guide you in forgiving your spouse?

When Jesus taught His disciples to pray, he used these words, *"forgive us our debts, as we also have forgiven our debtors"* (Matthew 6:12) or as Luke puts it "forgive us our sins, for we ourselves forgive everyone who is indebted to us" (Luke 11:4).

When we forgive others for their sins against us; we are canceling their sin debt to us. We are, in a sense, pardoning them and releasing our right to demand payment for their sin against us.

To biblically forgive means that we won't treat our offender as our indebted servant. We release our right to make them pay. We won't use their sin to shame or manipulate them. We won't treat them as if they owe us something.

Forgiving our spouse for their sexual sin is hard. Sin hurts! It is costly to forgive. We've only to look at the cross of Christ to see how much pain sin causes and how great the cost. But remember this, we do not pay the sin price from our own pocket. Christ has paid it forward! We forgive others out of the abundance of the forgiveness we have received in Jesus (Ephesians 1:7; Ephesians 4:32).

Question 2: Have you forgiven your spouse for their sin debt against you? Please share your thoughts.

_____

_____

_____

_____

Next, let's consider what forgiveness is *not* and answer some of the questions mentioned at the beginning of the lesson.

Forgiveness does not mean that we are okay with the sin.

God was not okay with our sin. He was filled with righteous anger and wrath at it. To His praise, Jesus stood in our place and drank the full cup of God's wrath against our sin (Matthew 26:39) so that we might drink the cup of fellowship with God and each other (1 John 1:3).

Because we are made in the image of God, we too will be angry at sin, but we must be careful. Ephesians 4:26-27 guides us to *"Be angry and do not sin; do not let the sun go down on your anger and give no opportunity to the devil."*

If we sin in our anger over the sin our spouse has committed, then we add insult to injury and are now in need of repentance ourselves. Instead of giving the devil an opportunity, we want to harness our righteous anger and use it to fuel our efforts to help our spouse overcome the devil's snares of lust and impurity.

Question 3: According to Ephesians 4:26-27, if we are sinfully angry toward our spouse, what are we doing?
- ☐ Teaching our spouse a lesson.
- ☐ Giving the devil an opportunity to harm us and our marriage.
- ☐ Standing up for our rights.

Forgiveness does not mean that we forget what happened.

When God forgives, He does not forget our sin; rather, He chooses to remember our sins no more (Hebrews 8:12). Instead of God remembering our sin, God remembers the perfect life Jesus lived for us in our place and the perfect sacrifice that Jesus made on the cross to pay for our sins. On this basis, He accepts us in Christ (Ephesians 1:6).

As much as we'd like to forget the sins we have committed, or our spouse has committed, we cannot. But we can consciously choose not to remember the sins, not to dwell on them, and not to talk with others about them in a vindictive way. We can overwhelm our negative thoughts about the sin with the good news of the gospel and the hope we have for our spouse's repentance and restoration. We will discuss this in more detail in future lessons.

> **Question 4:** Please fill in the blank: Hebrews 8:11-12 (NIV): "...
> they will all know me, from the least of them to the greatest. For
> I will forgive their wickedness and will _____ _____
> _____ _____ _____."

Forgiveness is not the absence of consequences for sin.

*Consider Hebrews 12:6: "For the Lord disciplines the one he loves
and chastises every son whom he receives."*

Because Christ paid your sin debt, there is no punishment left for you. However, as children of God, we should expect the discipline of our Father in Heaven if we fall into habitual sin (Hebrews 12:5-11).

We can see an example of this in the life of King David, the man after God's own heart (1 Samuel 13:14). Ensnared in lust, David committed adultery with Bathsheba, and then he had her husband Uriah killed in an attempt to cover up the sin. In response, God sent the prophet Nathan to explain that David's sin would be forgiven, but David would experience God's discipline (2 Samuel 12:1-15). *"Nathan said to David, "The Lord also has put away your sin; you shall not die.[14] Nevertheless, because by this deed you have utterly scorned the Lord, the child who is born to you shall die." (2 Samuel 12:13-14).*

It is God who disciplines. God determines the consequences; we spouses do not.

God will sometimes use the local governing authorities (police), employers, or local church authorities (pastors/elders) to bring about His discipline. However, at no point in Scripture, do we see Him instructing husbands or wives to determine the discipline for their spouse's sin.

Instead, we must entrust ourselves to God and follow His plan for encouraging our spouse toward repentance. God will determine the consequences necessary to bring our spouse back to the way of righteousness. We must not hinder the work of God by attempting to "help" God by handing out the consequences we think are appropriate.

> **Question 5:** Why is it important for you not to try to dictate the necessary discipline for your spouse?
>
> _____
>
> _____
>
> _____
>
> _____

We will close out this lesson by briefly addressing the issue of forgiveness and repentance.

Over the years, I've had many people say to me, "I would forgive, but my spouse isn't repentant." And when asked how they know that their spouse is not repentant, they respond with complaints that their spouse didn't seem sincere, they didn't cry over their sin, or with complaints that their spouse fell to sexual sin again. But this sort of reasoning is not biblical because it is not consistent with the gospel of Jesus Christ.

Look with me at Jesus' instruction to his disciples regarding forgiving one another:

"Pay attention to yourselves! If your brother sins, rebuke him, and if he repents, forgive him, and if he sins against you seven times in the day, and turns to you seven times, saying, 'I repent,' you must forgive him." Luke 17:3-4

If you talk with your spouse about their sin and they listen to you and seek your forgiveness, then this must be taken as evidence of their repentance. Jesus doesn't mention any requirement for emotion.

Also, this passage makes it clear that we should not expect the sin issue to resolve immediately. Jesus says, *"...if he sins against you seven times in the day"* making it clear that the offender may even repeat the offense many times on the same day, and we're still to forgive him.

Oh, friend, can you see the gospel here? We, dear one, are repeat offenders against God. Our God is so holy and perfect that even what seems to us a tiny sinful thought is a horrible offense to Him; and yet, no matter how many times a day we come to Him and say, "I'm sorry; please forgive me" He is faithful to receive us as forgiven because the blood Jesus shed on the cross paid for our every sin. How awesome is our God!

Considering what Jesus does for us, surely, we must forgive our spouse as often as needed, *not judging their hearts or their motives*, but rather responding according to gospel grace and forgiving them as we ourselves have been forgiven.

> **Question 6:** Based on Luke 17:3-4, is your spouse repentant? Please explain.

_____

_____

_____

_____

An unrepentant person is one who has been shown their sin and the truth of Scripture but refuses to acknowledge the sin and turn to God for forgiveness and restoration (1 John 1:6-10). Sadly, it does happen.

In such cases, we must remember Jesus' response to those who were sinning against Him as He hung on the cross, *"Father, forgive them; for they know not what they do" (Luke 23:34).* We pray for those who sin against us unrepentantly. We show love and *"do good"* to those who hate us (Luke 6:27) all the while, hoping that one day they will repent. Such situations are very trying, and you will need the love, support, and encouragement of the body of Christ to help you along the way.

This shows the extreme importance of remaining in the body of Christ—a local church—and allowing them to minister God's grace to you in your time of need.

Question 7: What are your final thoughts about today's lesson on forgiveness?

_____

_____

_____

_____

Faith in Christ

Welcome back to the A United Front course. I'm glad you are here.

For the past couple of lessons, we have been discussing biblical forgiveness. We've seen how important it is; what it is, and what it isn't. By way of reminder, we learned that because we have received mercy and been forgiven such a great debt of sin, God expects us to follow Him in extending mercy and forgiveness to others.

We also answered the question regarding how often we forgive. Please review Luke 17:3-4 NIV, *"So watch yourselves. If your brother or sister sins against you, rebuke them; and if they repent, forgive them. Even if they sin against you seven times in a day and seven times come back to you saying, 'I repent,' you must forgive them."*

> **Question 1:** According to Luke 17:3-4, how often are we to forgive our spouse if they repent?
> ☐ Seven times
> ☐ When they promise not to do the sin again
> ☐ Every time

It is a natural response of our flesh to defend ourselves, stand up for our rights, and to insist that offenses against us get punished. By nature, we like to have limits, i.e., "three strikes and you're out." And yet, the Bible tells us that as followers of Jesus, we are called and equipped to forgive every time someone asks. This is a hard truth.

Notice the disciples' response to Jesus' teaching on forgiveness. *"The apostles said to the Lord, "Increase our faith!" Luke 17:5*

Faith is a necessity to our life in Christ—we are saved *"by grace through faith"* (Ephesians 2:8), we *"live by faith"* (Romans 1:17) and Hebrews 11:6 tells us that *"without faith, it is impossible to please God."* We need faith for everything in our Christian life but especially to forgive as we have been forgiven because when we forgive repeatedly, we are following Christ and uniting with Him in His sufferings. To forgive is to let go of the offense and to trust God to make things right instead of requiring the offender to do it.

> **Question 2:** How is your faith today? Can you relate to the disciples' cry, *"Lord, increase our faith!"*? Please share your thoughts here:

We know we need faith to forgive as we have been forgiven, but this begs the question: how do we get the faith we need? This is the subject of our lesson today.

Please read Hebrews 12:1-2, *"Therefore, since we are surrounded by such a great cloud of witnesses, let us throw off everything that hinders and the sin that so easily entangles. And let us run with perseverance the race marked out for us, fixing our eyes on Jesus, the pioneer, and perfecter of faith. For the joy set before him, he endured the cross, scorning its shame, and sat down at the right hand of the throne of God."*

> **Question 3:** Who is the source of and "perfecter" of our faith according to Hebrews 12:1-2?
> ☐ The Church
> ☐ Jesus
> ☐ Our Spouse

If we want to be those who forgive as we have been forgiven, we need to ask Jesus for the faith to do it. Hebrews 12 tells us that Jesus creates faith in our hearts, and He sustains that faith until the end. There will be no faith apart from our receiving it from Christ. But the good news is that Jesus is not a reluctant or meager Provider (Philippians 4:19).

Jesus literally poured out His life for you on the cross to atone for your sins. He has forgiven you for a lifetime of sin. Mercy, grace and peace flow out to you in abundance from His cross. He has gone before you, paving the road on which you now "run your race." He joyfully and generously gives you everything you need to run the race He has set before you.

Jesus has not only shown you how to forgive by paying your sin debt, but He has given you His Spirit to strengthen and sustain you as you live in forgiveness with your spouse. When you look to Jesus for the faith you need, you always find it because Jesus is the Perfecter of your faith. He is the origin of your faith and the ongoing supply of it as well.

> **Question 4:** How does looking to Jesus give you the faith you need to live in forgiveness with your spouse?

My husband struggled mightily to break free from the snare of sexual impurity and in the early days of our journey to purity, there was a lot of forgiving that needed to happen.

I can remember being so weary of it all, lying on my face in my closet, crying my eyes out and begging God for help. "Lord, increase my faith. Please help me. Please help my husband. I believe that you are going to heal our marriage but help my unbelief. I just can't see how You are going to do it. Help me, Lord; give me faith to make it."

I was like the widow in 1 Kings 17:10-16, thinking all was lost. When the widow met the prophet Elijah, he asked her to feed him, but she said she couldn't do it. She told him that she was getting ready to make one last meal for her and her son, and then they would die from starvation. She had no faith. She was looking at what she had and saying, "It isn't enough. I can't do it. I have to take care of my son and myself."

But as usual, God had other plans. Elijah tells the woman, *"Don't be afraid..."* offer what you have to God, and He will sustain you and your son. And by grace, God enables this widow to step out in faith. She obeys and feeds Elijah first, and sure enough, her oil and flour never run out.

Friend, God is faithful. Even if you don't think you have the resources within you to forgive, God will give you the faith to do it. You don't have to trust your spouse; you only need to trust God.

I joyfully testify that Jesus enabled this in my life, He gave me faith to believe the message of the cross both for myself and for my husband, and I'm so thankful that He did. Today, my marriage is alive and strong because God enabled us to forgive each other as we have been forgiven.

So, coming to Jesus and looking to Him for the faith we need is the primary way to increase our faith, but God has also made other provisions for increasing our faith.

> **Question 5:** Please fill in the blanks. Romans 10:17, *"So _____ comes from _____, and hearing through the _____ of _____."*

We see in Romans 10 that faith comes by hearing the *"word of Christ"* which is the gospel.

Our faith is built up as we hear the message of the cross repeatedly. Earlier, we prayed for faith, and now we listen for the answer to our prayer by reading God's Word. We need to be actively preaching the gospel to ourselves by reading our Bibles, looking for the gospel, and then applying the gospel.

I remember reading and finding so much hope in these simple words from 2 Thessalonians 3:3, *"But the Lord is faithful. He will establish you and guard you against the evil one."* I read that verse and thought, "Yes! God has been faithful in the past; He will be faithful always. He sent Jesus to die on the cross, providing a way of salvation for me. Jesus has overcome sin, death, and hell and risen victorious; I am safe in Him. God did not bring me this far only to abandon me. I just need to wait on God to do the work He is doing in my marriage."

My marriage appeared dead and without hope, but through His Word, God said, "Trust me; I'm faithful; I will guard you and establish your marriage on Christ."

This good word brought peace to my heart and mind, and I stored that promise away in my heart to remember on days when I was struggling. I even wrote it down on a card and stuck it to my refrigerator to help me remember.

But, dear friend, I would have never received my encouragement if I had not been reading my Bible. If you want your faith to grow, then you must read the Bible so that you can hear from the Giver of faith.

I like the way the New Living Translation of Colossians 2:7 puts it, *"Let your roots grow down into him and draw up nourishment from him, so you will grow in faith, strong and vigorous in the truth you were taught. Let your lives overflow with thanksgiving for all he has done."*

We must be in the Word of God so that our roots can grow down into Christ where we will be able to draw up nourishment for our souls and our faith will grow strong!

Question 6: Are you reading your Bible regularly to hear from God?
☐ Yes
☐ No
☐ I have questions about this topic.

Another way for us to have our faith built up is for us to hear the gospel taught, preached and sung at our local church.

Hebrews 10:24-25 guides us in this regard: *"And let us consider how we may spur one another on toward love and good deeds,²⁵ not giving up meeting together, as some are in the habit of doing, but encouraging one another—and all the more as you see the Day approaching."*

We can see here that this "giving up" on meeting with other believers is a common struggle. Sexual impurity in a marriage fosters isolation, but we must resist the desire to shut ourselves off from the body of Christ.

By His death and resurrection, Jesus has removed all barriers between us and God; we are safe in Him our High Priest. Therefore, we can, and we should draw near to Him (Hebrews 10:19-23), but we aren't meant to always do this privately. God has a purpose in having His people gather together.

When we come together corporately as a body of believers to worship our Lord, we have the opportunity to be served and to serve others, to encourage others and be encouraged toward love and good deeds.

Mike and I did not have a local church when we first started out, but God led us to one quickly. It was there that we found the guidance, love, and counsel that set us on the path to gospel freedom.

If you and your spouse don't go to church, you will miss out on being encouraged in the gospel. And you will deny yourselves the encouragement, love and the help of other believers.

> **Question 7:** Are you and your spouse being encouraged through your local church? Please share.

_____

_____

_____

_____

As you pass through this trial, you might be called, as I was, to forgive repeatedly. The devil is never happy to see captives freed from his trap of impurity, and he will do all he can to cause you and your husband to stumble and fall back into the pit of lust or the snare of despair, so don't be surprised if things seem to get worse before they get better. But remember, God is with you and He will give you the faith you need to forgive as He has forgiven you.

LESSON 8:

Gospel Counsel

*H*ello and welcome back to the A United Front! I hope that you are finding these lessons helpful.

In lesson seven, we learned the role of faith in our goal of becoming a united front with our spouse against the schemes of the devil. We discussed some ways to increase our faith—prayer, preaching the gospel to ourselves, and hearing the gospel preached at our local church.

Today, we want to look at another way in which we might listen to the gospel and learn to apply it, and that is through gospel-focused counseling.

Just as we might go to a doctor when we are persistently feeling unwell, there are times when we will benefit from seeking counsel for our marriage. And while it can be helpful to have someone speak life and hope into our situation, as Christians, we must be selective about the counsel we seek.

You might be familiar with support groups, psychology, life coaches, or therapy; these are all concepts and theoretical approaches which the world has devised to deal with the problem of sin. However, since the world is without faith in Christ and blinded to the truth of God's Word, their counsel will always be short-sighted and limited to the power of the counselee's will. Worldly counsel is like putting a bandage on a life-threatening wound; it is insufficient.

The good news is that for us who have put our faith in Jesus, there is a *"more excellent way"* (1 Corinthians 12:31)—the gospel way. In Christ, we have the Way, the Truth, and the Life (John 14:6). We are united to Christ and share fellowship with Him (Romans 6:4-9; 1 Corinthians 1:2-4, 9). Because God has cleansed us from sin and made us righteous through Jesus' death on the cross, we can be confident that He will continue to transform us by His grace (2 Corinthians 3:18).

In Jesus, we have received all that we need for life and godliness (John 1:1; 2 Peter 1:3) including the power of the cross which both saves and sanctifies us and our spouse (1 Corinthians 1:18). We are not dependent on our strength but instead, we rely on the power of God working in us (Philippians 2:13), and He is mighty to save (Zephaniah 3:17)! Gospel counseling is the counsel that we need.

Question 1: Have you received local counseling for yourself or your marriage? Please share.

_____

_____

_____

_____

In times of crisis, we might be tempted to combine the gospel counsel found in Jesus with man's wisdom. We might reason that since our case is dire, we could benefit from both secular counsel and gospel counsel, but we would be wrong to think this way.

Trying to combine the wisdom of man and the counsel of the gospel is like trying to harmonize light with darkness (2 Corinthians 6:15). It doesn't work. At some point, the two counsels will contradict and even wholly oppose each other, which will not only be confusing but also detrimental to your situation.

The conflict between the wisdom of man and the gospel is not new. When writing to the church at Corinth—a church fraught with all kinds of sin problems including sexual impurity—Paul wrote:

> *"For the word of the cross is folly to those who are perishing, but to us who are being saved, it is the power of God. For it is written, "I will destroy the wisdom of the wise, and the discernment of the discerning I will thwart." Where is the one who is wise? Where is the scribe? Where is the debater of this age? Has not God made foolish the wisdom of the world?" 1 Corinthians 1:18-20*

Question 2: What is the "word of the cross" to those who are being saved?

- ☐ It is folly.
- ☐ It is not enough.
- ☐ It is the power of God.

From the beginning, the devil has tried to cast doubt on the sufficiency of God and His Word for His people. In the garden of Eden, Satan met up with Eve and began the conversation with, *"Did God really say..."* And in the end, Eve was deceived into thinking that there was wisdom to be gained by eating from the tree of knowledge of good and evil (Genesis 3:6).

And many years later in the desert as he was tempting Christ, Satan tried the same tactic with the words, *"If you are the Son of God..."* But Jesus was not deceived. He succeeded where Adam and Eve and humans throughout time have failed. He thwarted Satan with these words, *"It is written, 'Man shall not live by bread alone, but by every word that comes from the mouth of God.'"*

Now notice this from Hebrews 1:1-2, *"Long ago, at many times and in many ways, God spoke to our fathers by the prophets,[2] but in these last days he has spoken to us by his Son, whom he appointed the heir of all things, through whom also he created the world..."*

Question 3: According to Hebrews 1:2, how has God spoken to us? Fill in the blank. "In these last days, he has _____ to us by his _____..."

Dear friend, God has not withheld from us anything we need in His Word (2 Peter 1:3). We might be tempted to think we need something more, but we don't. Jesus and His gospel completely and fully address every need that we have. Jesus and His gospel are God's final word.

And the message that Jesus communicates is one of resounding mercy, love, and grace. If you will listen and apply Jesus' message to your life, you will be transformed. Worldly counsel can make no such promises.

For example, when I look to the cross of Jesus, I see Jesus dying for my sins, which gives me a new outlook on my life. The cross tells me that I am a sinner in need of a Savior; this is humbling, but it helps me to abandon sinful anger about my husband's sin and self-pity. When I consider the resurrection of Jesus, I rejoice that sin no longer has controlling power in my life and my husband's life. Jesus has overcome for us, and He gives me hope that I can have a marriage that is free from sexual impurity and fully restored. Thinking about this removes my despair and fear that my life will never change. Do you see the value of and the hope that gospel counsel provides?

> **Question 4:** As you consider the death and resurrection of Jesus today, how does it affect your heart and your attitude toward your spouse?

_____

_____

_____

_____

Briefly, I want to show you a biblical illustration of gospel counsel in action within a local church. Paul writes to the church in Corinth:

> *"It is actually reported that there is sexual immorality among you, and of a kind that is not tolerated even among pagans, for a man has his father's wife. And you are arrogant! Ought you not rather to mourn? Let him who has done this be removed from among you. For though absent in body, I am present in spirit; and as if present, I have already pronounced judgment on the one who did such a thing. When you are assembled in the name of the Lord Jesus and my spirit is present, with the power of our Lord Jesus, you are to deliver this man to Satan for the destruction of the flesh, so that his spirit may be saved in the day of the Lord."*
> *1 Corinthians 5:1-5*

The situation was this: there was a man in the Corinthian church who was unrepentantly and openly having an immoral relationship with his stepmother. Paul got word of this and wrote to the local church with instructions on what to do.

Question 5: According to 1 Corinthians 5:4-5, what did Paul tell the Corinthians to do about the immorality in the church?

- ☐ Hand the man over to Satan (put him out of the church)
- ☐ Overlook it
- ☐ Give the man communion

This situation in Corinth was serious; this man was openly flaunting his immorality. Maybe your marriage feels as problematic as this circumstance in Corinth, but if so, be encouraged, there is hope. God had a plan for the recovery of this man.

Paul told the Corinthian believers to gather together in the name of Jesus and the power of Christ and deliver the man over to Satan by putting the man out of the church. Essentially this is step 3 of Matthew 18, which we studied in a previous lesson; due to the openness of the immorality, the process accelerated quickly.

Question 6: According to 1 Corinthians 5:5, what was the purpose of handing the man over to Satan?

- ☐ So that the man would be punished for his sins.
- ☐ So that the man would be ashamed and leave town.
- ☐ So that the man's spirit might be saved by Jesus.

Notice what Paul did not say; Paul did not say, "Hand the man over to Satan, so he will get what he deserves." Paul's goal was gospel-focused: this man's salvation. The "handing over" was so that Jesus might save the man's spirit.

Gospel-focused counsel is restorative, not punitive. The goal of gospel counsel is that the sinful individual might realize their need for Jesus and return to their local body of believers washed and cleansed by the Lord Jesus.

Now, let's read the conclusion of the matter and Paul's additional counsel to the body of Corinth in 2 Corinthians 2:5-11:

> *"Now if anyone has caused pain, he has caused it not to me, but in some measure—not to put it too severely—to all of you. For such a one, this punishment by the majority is enough, so you should rather turn to forgive and comfort him, or he may be*

overwhelmed by excessive sorrow. So, I beg you to reaffirm your love for him. For this is why I wrote that I might test you and know whether you are obedient in everything. Anyone whom you forgive, I also forgive. Indeed, what I have forgiven, if I have forgiven anything, has been for your sake in the presence of Christ, so that we would not be outwitted by Satan; for we are not ignorant of his designs."

This situation at Corinth caused a lot of grief to Paul and to the body of believers in Corinth, but it is evident from Paul's additional counsel (to forgive, love and restore to fellowship) that the immoral man repented and desired to be restored to the body of Christ. And this is what gospel counsel is all about—forgiveness, love, and restoration through Jesus.

Gospel counsel is counsel that has the message of restoration through the atoning death of Jesus Christ at the heart of it. It is counsel that continually points us to the blood Jesus shed to redeem us, the death Jesus died to forgive us, and the resurrection of Jesus to provide us a new heart and life. It is counsel that brings a believing person (couple) to the cross and the empty tomb of Jesus so they might understand the implications and experience the benefits of this good news in their life and marriage.

Question 7: Do you have any thoughts or questions about gospel counsel? Please share.

_____

_____

_____

_____

An Important Question

*H*ello, friend, and welcome back to the A United Front course.

In lesson eight, we saw the significance of seeking out gospel counsel. Today, we will ask an important question that will hopefully be both enlightening and helpful to you on your way to becoming a united front with your spouse.

Let's begin by reading Jesus' counsel to a man whose issues were so heavy that they kept him immobilized for over 38 years.

> *"When Jesus saw him lying there and knew that he had already been there a long time, he said to him, "Do you want to be healed?" The sick man answered him, "Sir, I have no one to put me into the pool when the water is stirred up, and while I am going another steps down before me." Jesus said to him, "Get up, take up your bed, and walk." And at once the man was healed, and he took up his bed and walked. Now that day was the Sabbath. So, the Jews said to the man who had been healed, "It is the Sabbath, and it is not lawful for you to take up your bed." But he answered them, "The man who healed me, that man said to me, 'Take up your bed, and walk.'" They asked him, "Who is the man who said to you, 'Take up your bed and walk'?" Now the man who had been healed did not know who it was, for Jesus had withdrawn, as there was a crowd in the place. Afterward, Jesus found him in the temple and said to him, "See, you are well! Sin no more, that nothing worse may happen to you." John 5:6-14*

In Jesus' day, there was a traditional belief that an angel would come and periodically stir up the waters of the pool of Bethesda in Jerusalem and anyone who entered the pool at the time the waters were stirred would be healed. So, infirmed people from all around the region would go there for healing, and this is the setting for our passage.

So, Jesus walked into the midst of a multitude of blind, lame and paralyzed people, but He directed His attention to one man. And Jesus doesn't offer this man pity or assistance, instead, he asks the man a question.

> **Question 1:** What is the question that Jesus asks the man? Fill in the blank: Jesus *said to him, "Do you* _____ *to be* _____*?"*

We might initially be surprised by Jesus' question, but we get insight into why Jesus asked it from the admonition Jesus gives to the man later that day. Jesus said to the man, *"See, you are well again. Stop sinning or something worse may happen to you."*

It appears that this man's malady, from which he suffered for 38 years, was sin related. Sin (our own and other's) makes us heart sick, but sometimes, it also makes us physically sick (Psalm 38). When my marriage was in crisis, my husband and I both felt emotionally, physically and spiritually ill.

So, Jesus sees the man and addresses his sin sick heart with a challenge of sorts. *"Do you want to be healed?"* It's as if Jesus is saying, *"I see your heart issue, and I can heal you, but are you going to cooperate?"*

> **Question 2:** Please answer Jesus' question as it relates to your situation. Do you want your heart and your marriage to be healed by Jesus?
> ☐ Yes
> ☐ No
> ☐ I have questions about this topic

Now notice how the sick man answered Jesus' question. Instead of a resounding, "Yes, I want to be healed!" this sick man reports, *"I have no one to help me. I try, but others get in my way."*

Question 3: Has anything hindered you or kept you from your healing? Please share.

_____

_____

_____

_____

Perhaps you think that the only hindrance to your healing is your spouse and their sin struggles. But, dear friend, there are usually additional issues in the marriage. There are heart issues—yours and your spouse' s—which must be addressed by Jesus for healing to come.

As we have seen in previous lessons, we are all sinners in need of salvation and sanctification. We cannot force our spouse to accept Christ or to repent, but neither can we blame them for our sin issues. One person's sin does not excuse another's.

The good news is that there is healing for you and your marriage in Jesus. Even if you or your husband do not fully comprehend your need for healing, Jesus knows. Only Jesus has experienced all temptation (Hebrews 4:15), became sin itself (2 Corinthians 5:21), died and rose again overcoming sin, death, and hell on our behalf (Revelation 12:11). Only Jesus can truly comprehend the sickness (spiritual, physical, mental, emotional) of all people. You need not fear Jesus or His healing, but it might not come in the way you expect.

Notice that the healing of the sick man in John 5 does not happen the way he thought it would. From his conversation with Jesus, we can see that this man was fixed on the idea that his healing would come by him getting into the pool of Bethesda at just the right time. Never mind that he had been there for 38 years, and he still wasn't healed.

But we shouldn't think ourselves any better; we've all had the wrong focus or solution in hand at one point or another in our lives. I can remember having a hurting heart and repeatedly turning to chips, cookies, chocolate, etc. for comfort. There was another season when I turned to Christian psychological counseling for healing. I could go on listing false sources that lured me but suffice it to say that every time I came away worse than before I started.

Question 4: Have you tried methods other than the gospel of Jesus Christ for healing? Tell us about it here.

_____

_____

_____

_____

The world offers us a plethora of solutions for healing, but sadly, the world's cures will always leave us empty and wanting. But the good news is that God has made a way for us that is higher, wiser and sufficient to the need (Isaiah 55:8-9).

And what is this higher and better way of healing that God has provided? 1 Peter 2:22-25 tells us:

> _He committed no sin, neither was deceit found in his mouth. When he was reviled, he did not revile in return; when he suffered, he did not threaten but continued entrusting himself to him who judges justly. He himself bore our sins in his body on the tree, that we might die to sin and live to righteousness._ **_By his wounds, you have been healed._** _For you were straying like sheep but have now returned to the Shepherd and Overseer of your souls._ (1 Peter 2:22-25)

By Jesus' wounds, we have been healed. Jesus bore your sin, took your punishment, and suffered your death that you might be forgiven, justified and sanctified. If you want to be healed, the healing is yours, but you must look to Jesus and follow Him if you want to experience it.

Question 5: Considering 1 Peter 2:22-25, how do you feel about Christ and all that He endured to secure healing for you and your husband?

_____

_____

_____

_____

What a great Savior we have! He is worthy of our praise and worship! He loves you very much, dear friend.

Now, let us return to our passage and consider how Jesus heals the man.

> *"Jesus said to him, 'Get up, take up your bed, and walk.' And at once the man was healed, and he took up his bed and walked."*
> *John 5:8-9*

Jesus said: *"Get up, take your bed and walk."* and the man got up, took his bed and walked. It is almost shockingly immediate, isn't it? No discussion; no arguments, no excuses. Jesus said, "Get up and go" and the man got up and went. The man was completely healed!

Many spouses have come to Setting Captives Free and said that they wanted healing from Jesus; however, when the gospel counsel given to them was something that they did not want to do, they halted. This is akin to the sick man saying to Jesus, "Oh, sorry, I can't pick up my mat and walk; that's the one thing I can't do."

Here are a few examples of gospel counsel that are sometimes refused:

- Involve someone local to you (pastor, teacher, elder, gospel counselor, etc.)
- Attend a gospel-centered church
- Spend more time with your spouse
- Forgive your spouse
- Bless your spouse

Counsel such as the above has been rejected, for one reason or another, by people who were unwilling to obey Jesus and His gospel. Some were afraid of the unknown. Some were worried about being embarrassed. Some were worried their spouse would lose their job or go to jail. Some had just grown accustomed or numb to their situation. Regardless of the faulty reasoning, none of these individuals found healing for their hearts because they refused to do what needed doing.

Friend, you cannot experience the healing that Jesus has for you if you are unwilling to step out in faith and do what He tells you to do.

"So also, faith by itself, if it does not have works, is dead." James 2:17

Question 6: Based on James 2:17, would you say that your faith is living or dead? Please share.

_____

_____

_____

_____

I hope that you are one who wants to be healed and that your faith in Jesus and His gospel is living and vibrant, which will motivate you to do what you need to do to experience your healing. But if you are struggling, then I urge you to come back for the next lesson and more gospel encouragement. As you continue to hear the gospel and believe it, your faith will grow stronger. I'm praying for you.

Living as New Creations in Christ

*G*reetings and welcome back to the A United Front course. I pray that your return today means that you are willing to do whatever it takes to receive the healing which is in Jesus.

In this lesson and the next, we will be seeking the Lord together for the foundational and motivating understanding we need to live as people who have been healed by Jesus.

Perhaps like me, you have many different roles to fill—spouse, parent, friend, employee, volunteer, etc. Such titles or labels can be useful in organizing our world, but *sometimes we can get so focused on our temporal identities that we lose sight of our eternal duty*, and this can be harmful to our hearts and relationships.

When my husband and I began our healing journey, I felt adrift on a sea of emotional turmoil. I did not respond to my husband's sin in faith as a child of God. I responded to my circumstances based on my feelings and fears as a wounded wife and frightened mother.

I felt like a failure as a wife thinking that if only, I had been a better, smarter, or prettier wife then my husband wouldn't have been tempted toward sexual sin. I feared that my husband was an addict who would never really change, but at the same time, I wanted our children to have a father, so I tried to regulate my husband's activity and guilt him into repentance.

Question 1: Can you relate to the struggle I had with responding to my husband based on my fears and feelings? Please share.

_____

_____

_____

_____

If we want to stand up against the temptations to respond to our circumstances based on our temporary identities instead of our eternal one, we must learn the truth about who we are in Christ so that it can dominate our thinking. To do this, let's look together at 2 Corinthians 5:14-21. We will look at the first half of this passage today, and then finish the second half tomorrow.

> *"For the love of Christ controls us, because we have concluded this: that one has died for all, therefore all have died; and he died for all, that those who live might no longer live for themselves but for him who for their sake died and was raised From now on, therefore, we regard no one according to the flesh. Even though we once regarded Christ according to the flesh, we regard him thus no longer. Therefore, if anyone is in Christ, he is a new creation. The old has passed away; behold, the new has come. All this is from God, who through Christ reconciled us to himself and gave us the ministry of reconciliation; that is, in Christ God was reconciling the world to himself, not counting their trespasses against them, and entrusting to us the message of reconciliation. Therefore, we are ambassadors for Christ, God making his appeal through us. We implore you on behalf of Christ, be reconciled to God. For our sake he made him to be sin who knew no sin so that in him we might become the righteousness of God."*

Question 2: According to 2 Corinthians 5:14, what does Paul describe as his compelling motivation in life? Fill in the blank.

"For the _____ _____ _____ controls us..."

It is the love of Christ that compels and should control all believers! So, the first thing we can know about who we are in Christ is that we are loved. And this love is not temporary or faltering as human love might be. No! God loves us with an eternal and unchanging love that is so great that nothing can separate us from it (Romans 8:35-39). The cross of Jesus Christ is absolute proof of this truth (see John 13:1 and 1 John 3:16).

Question 3: According to 2 Corinthians 5:14-15, what was it that convinced Paul that Christ loved him?
- ☐ The easy life that God had given to Paul.
- ☐ The good relationships that Paul enjoyed.
- ☐ The death and resurrection of Jesus for us all.

Jesus' death on the cross was the proof of His love for us all.

Out of love, God sent His only Son, Jesus, into the world, not to condemn you but to save you. Christ suffered and died an agonizing death to give you life eternal and abundant. Jesus' loving heart was pierced for your sake to fill your heart with His everlasting love (Romans 5:5). And He rose again to give you a new life in Him.

It is His divine, heart flooding love with which you are loved that is to control you as you live your new life in Jesus. The love of Jesus compels you, friend, to love and forgive those who have sinned against you, and to look at them not according to the flesh but according to the Spirit (2 Corinthians 5:16).

Question 4: Pause and consider the cross of Jesus Christ. What thoughts do you have when you consider the love of God as manifested in Jesus' death for you? Please share them here:

_____

_____

_____

_____

I have tears running down my face as I write about and consider this amazing cross, this wondrous, life-giving love that God has poured out on us. As we believe in Christ and all that He has done on our behalf, how can we not fall to our knees in gratitude? Our Jesus took off His royal robes to clothe Himself in humanity and live among us, but we despised and rejected Him. We crucified the Lord of Glory by our sin, unbelief, and rebellion, but did He stomp off mad or throw us into Hell? No! He rose again, came back, and blessed us with His Spirit, and He lives today interceding for us and is soon to take us to heaven!

Does this affect your heart, dear friend? If so, then let the truth of the cross both flood your heart and dominate your mind today, and let it be the controlling force in your life. This is God's will for you.

> _"and he died for all, that those who live might no longer live for themselves but for him who for their sake died and was raised. From now on, therefore, we regard no one according to the flesh. Even though we once regarded Christ according to the flesh, we regard him thus no longer." 2 Corinthians 5:15-16_

Paul is speaking to the Corinthians so powerfully because he had experienced this great change in his own life. Paul once viewed Christ and His followers as those who should be persecuted and put to death (2 Corinthians 5:16), but then he "saw the Light" (Acts 22:6). He was cut in his heart at the sight of the cross and healed by Jesus' love and power, and then his whole viewpoint changed (Acts 9:1-22). After he received Jesus' love, Paul gladly identified himself as belonging to Christ. He looked at everyone with eyes of love and hope, knowing that if Christ could change *him* then there was hope for all.

> **Question 5:** Considering how Christ loved you at the cross, how does this help you to respond to your spouse and their sin struggles differently?

_____

_____

_____

_____

Now we can see the power of finding our identity in Christ and His love. When we see how deeply loved we are, then we are able to live differently.

Because Jesus loved us so much that He suffered and died for us, now in response, we should not live for ourselves but for Him who died for us. This is what it means to live out the gospel.

This truth hit me like a ton of bricks the first time I understood it. Those words *"might no longer live for themselves"* penetrated my heart, because as I surveyed the history of my life, I saw that I had been living for myself. Not in every way, I served my family daily, but my selfishness showed up in how I responded to my husband and children, and how I reacted to their sin struggles.

I pray that as you contemplate the cross today that God's amazing love is affecting your heart, and that you see your situation and yourself with new eyes full of love and hope. I also pray that you are coming to know how you are able, by the power of the Holy Spirit living in you, to no longer live for yourself but instead to live for Him Who died for you.

> **Question 6:** Please fill in the blank. "Therefore, if _____ is in Christ, he is a _____ _____. The _____has passed away; behold, the _____ has come." 2 Corinthians 5:17

Paul is making a significant point here, so he anchors the eternal truth to its Source. The phrase "in Christ" is an expression used over three hundred times in the New Testament, and every time it is used it refers to an essential truth about our relationship with or identity in Christ.

Before Christ, in our natural selves, we were self-centered, self-protective, angry, fearful, and living for ourselves. But now in Christ, we are new creations—all things have become new. We have Holy Spirit power to live differently. We can now have an attitude of hope and joy and a loving, eternally minded perspective on our life. We have a new heart that can love and value others more than ourselves, and a spirit that desires reconciliation. We are moving from living for ourselves to living for Him Who died for us. We are *"new creations."*

Let's close out our lesson by making a summary of what we have learned. We have seen that God loves us. Paul took us to the cross as proof of God's love, because it was at the cross that Jesus poured out His life unto death for us, to forgive our sins and pardon us and reconcile us to God. And this incredible love of Christ, exhibited on the cross, is the compelling factor in the lives of all believers.

We understood the importance of no longer seeing and judging ourselves or others according to the flesh but instead we base our understanding and responses on who Christ has made us to be by His death and resurrection, and the infilling of His Holy Spirit.

And finally, we have seen our identity as those who are new creations in Christ. Our old selfish life, our self-protectiveness, and our self-motivation all died on the cross with Christ, and we rose with Him to a new life. Motivated by the love of Christ, we can turn from selfish living to living for the One Who died for us.

Question 7: What does it mean to be a new creation in Christ? Please share your thoughts:

_____

_____

_____

_____

I hope your heart has been thoroughly encouraged to see how deeply loved you are by Jesus and that your mind has been renewed by finding your identity in Christ and not in your fears and feelings as a spouse. I'm praying for you and look forward to seeing you in the next lesson where we will complete our study in 2 Corinthians 5.

Reconciled Reconcilers

$\mathcal{T}$oday, we're continuing our study of our identity in Christ.

As a quick review, we saw in lesson ten that God deeply loves us and that through the death and resurrection of Jesus, all who believe are new creations in Christ. We understood that as new creations in Christ, we are not to live for ourselves, but instead, we are to live for Jesus Who died for us. And as we live for Jesus, we will respond to our spouse's sins against us in a gospel way instead of according to our fears and feelings.

As we begin today, let's start by reading 2 Corinthians 5:18-21:

> *All this is from God, who through Christ reconciled us to himself and gave us the ministry of reconciliation; that is, in Christ God was reconciling the world to himself, not counting their trespasses against them, and entrusting to us the message of reconciliation. Therefore, we are ambassadors for Christ, God making his appeal through us. We implore you on behalf of Christ, be reconciled to God.²¹ For our sake he made him to be sin who knew no sin so that in him we might become the righteousness of God.*'

Question 1: According to 2 Corinthians 5:18, what did God do for us? Fill in the blank. "*All this is from _____, who through _____ _____ us to himself...*"

Reconciliation is such a beautiful word, isn't it? It means "the restoration of friendly relations." And this is what God has done for us through Jesus!

Sin came into the world and separated us from God, making us His enemies (Romans 5:10). But in His vast mercy and love, God has reconciled us to Himself through the cross of Jesus Christ! Through Jesus' death on the cross, He removed the sin barrier that prevented us from having a relationship with Him. Now, we "rejoice in God through our Lord Jesus Christ, through whom we have received reconciliation" (Romans 5:11). The cross has made enemies into friends.

Oh, friend, our identity is not found in our past or present circumstances! If we have put our faith in Jesus, we are those who are in Christ *reconciled to God* at the cross.

As a believer in Jesus, you now have God as your Friend—the best Friend ever! He knows you fully and loves you deeply. He never wearies of your voice or ignores your call. He never sleeps, is never too busy, and the words He speaks to you will always be perfect.

> **Question 2:** What does it mean that you have been reconciled to God? Please share your thoughts.
>
> _____
>
> _____
>
> _____
>
> _____

> **Question 3:** According to 2 Corinthians 5:18-19, when God reconciled you to Himself through Jesus, He also gave you a ministry. What is this ministry?
> - ☐ The ministry of wellness
> - ☐ The ministry of reconciliation
> - ☐ The ministry of justice

If you are a believer in Jesus Christ, you have a ministry of reconciliation. Reconciled and reconciling; this is our identity in Christ.

Jesus came not only to reconcile you to God but also to reconcile us one to another. We are to reconcile with others whenever possible (Romans 12:18) and to encourage others to be reconciled to God through the gospel (2 Corinthians 5:20).

And this is what we are doing when we speak with our spouse about their sin and invite them to repent. We are essentially saying, "I love you, and so I want you to be right with God and with me. Please turn from your sin and receive the love and forgiveness that are yours through the death of Jesus on the cross."

The foundation for your reconciliation with God and your spouse is the gospel of Jesus Christ. Through Jesus, your relationship with God has been made right. Jesus has made peace with God for you. And now, Jesus comes to you and your spouse, and He says, "I died to cover and forgive your sins with my shed blood. You are forgiven, and you can forgive. By my wounds, your relationship is healed. I have reconciled you to God, now reconcile with each other based on what I have done for you and what I am doing in you."

> **Question 4:** In 2 Corinthians 5:19, we see that there is some-
> thing God did not hold against us? Please fill in the blank.
> *"in Christ God was reconciling the world to himself, _____*
> *_____ _____ _____ against them,"*

God did not count our trespasses against us, and the reason that God does not count our sins against us is that He counted them against His Son instead. God counted His innocent Son Jesus as guilty in our place so that we who were sinful might be righteous.

God does not love and accept you because you are good. You are not reconciled to God by your efforts but through the finished work of Jesus Christ on the cross. God loves and treats you as His friend because Christ has removed the sin barrier that once stood between you and the Father. And even though you still sin, God loves you and treats you as His beloved child because you have been reconciled to God through Jesus' death on the cross.

And this is the mindset that we need to have in our marriages. We should not mistreat our spouse when they sin against us. We are to forgive and make every effort to reconcile because this is what God has done for us. And while it isn't always possible to be reconciled with others, as children of God, we can try.

This truth was hard for me to accept in the beginning days. I felt so betrayed and hurt that I didn't think that I could let go of the pain. But when I read this passage, I realized I had a wrong perspective. I had forgotten what Christ had done for me (2 Peter 1:9) and was not only holding my husband's sins against him but also treating him according to his sins. Sometimes I was subtle about it by denying small kindnesses, and other times, I was openly punitive. I would speak to my husband in a way that I knew would wound him, or I would remind him of his sin and how much it hurt me.

As I began to remember what God had done for me through Jesus, I realized that as long as I was counting my husband's sins against him, I was sinning. How could I hold my husband's sins against him when God did not hold my sins against me? I was not a reconciler, and I needed to repent of it.

I remember praying something like this:

> *"Father in Heaven, I see that you did not count my sins against me but against Your Own Son, Jesus Christ. Please forgive me for my sin of counting my husband's sins against him and help me to forgive from my heart and love my husband as You have loved me."*

Oh, the joy and relief that flooded my soul as I repented to the Lord and released my husband's sins to God! It was as if a weight was lifted from my heart, and I began to treat my husband with the abundant mercy and love that I had received from Jesus. It was a significant turning point in our journey to healing.

Question 5: Have you been holding your spouse's sins against them? If so, please feel free to write out a prayer of repentance as I did or just share your thoughts.

_____

_____

_____

_____

If you are struggling with this concept, I am sympathetic, but allow me to comfort you with the gospel truth. You are not alone. If you are a believer, you are in Christ (1 Corinthians 1:30), and Christ is in you (Romans 8:10). You have everything you need for life and godliness (2 Peter 1:3) because of Jesus' death and resurrection. God has already given you Jesus; He will not withhold anything helpful or necessary from you (Psalm 84:11; Romans 8:32). Look to Jesus in faith, and He will enable you by His grace to move forward in your ministry of reconciliation with your spouse.

Question 6: What is the title that God has given to us in 2 Corinthians 5:20?
- ☐ Ambassadors for Christ
- ☐ Accountants for Christ
- ☐ Allies for Christ

Because we are reconciled to God through Jesus' death and resurrection, and we have a ministry of reconciliation, we are ambassadors for Christ! We represent God, showing His love and forgiveness to others.

And as ambassadors for Christ, we must encourage others (especially our spouse) to be reconciled to God. We evidence that we are God's ambassadors when we call others to be reconciled to God in Christ. And one way we can do this is to share the gospel with our spouse and to forgive them as we have been forgiven.

As you remind yourself and your spouse of Christ's finished work on the cross, and the new and true identity you both have in Christ, then there is real hope that you will both turn away from the deeds of the flesh and instead walk according to the Spirit, living in purity and love with each other.

As ambassadors for Christ, we come to our spouse and speak the words of 2 Corinthians 5:21, "*For our sake he made him to be sin who knew no sin so that in him we might become the righteousness of God.*"

Oh, friend, this great exchange (Christ's righteousness for our sin) took place at the cross, and it is what makes our reconciliation with God and others possible.

Not only did Jesus take your sins on Himself, but He literally became sin for you so that you might become the righteousness of God in Him. Because Jesus took your sin and gave you His righteousness, you are considered righteous in God's eyes. And if your spouse has placed their faith in Christ, this is true for them too. This is good news for your heart and your spouse!

Lesson 11: Reconciled Reconcilers

It is in Christ and His righteousness that you and your believing spouse will find your true identity:

- You are loved by God, a new creation in Christ, ambassadors of Christ and completely holy and righteous in God's eyes.
- You are not sinners trying to do better, but saints who sometimes stumble and sin.
- You are not seeking God's approval; you are already pleasing and accepted by God because you are in Christ.
- You are holy because Jesus took your sin and clothed you with His righteousness.

> **Question 7:** Please list some ways in which you have been or can be an ambassador for Christ to your spouse.
>
> _____
>
> _____
>
> _____
>
> _____

Embrace your true identity in Christ, and it will change the way you live and interact with your spouse and everyone else in your life.

Who is to Blame?

I have heard some people teach that if we pursue our spouse sexually enough, then our spouse will never be tempted to view pornography or commit adultery; however, we do not find this assurance taught in Scripture.

Certainly, we are all called to be good stewards of our bodies (1 Corinthians 6:12-20; Romans 12: 1-8) and to do all we can to "quench" the burning of our spouse (1 Corinthians 7), this topic is addressed in later lessons, but today we want to understand the futility of assigning blame and to learn the biblical response to it when it happens.

To see this, let us consider the conversation between God and Adam in the Garden of Eden shortly after sin marred our world.

> *"But the Lord God called to the man and said to him, "Where are you?" And he said, "I heard the sound of you in the garden, and I was afraid, because I was naked, and I hid myself." He said, "Who told you that you were naked? Have you eaten of the tree of which I commanded you not to eat?" The man said, "The woman whom you gave to be with me, she gave me fruit of the tree, and I ate." Genesis 3:9-12*

Question 1: In Genesis 3:11, God asked Adam a question. Please fill in the blank. "Have you _____of the tree of which I _____ you _____ to eat?"

God created and then placed Adam and Eve in the Garden of Eden and told them to enjoy everything except one tree—the Tree of the Knowledge of Good and Evil. Then Satan came along and tempted Eve to eat of the forbidden tree.

Deceived, Eve ate the forbidden fruit and gave some to Adam, and he also ate. Sin entered the world.

I have always been intrigued by the conversation between God, Adam, Eve, and Satan. God knew what had transpired, but He asked Adam and Eve for their version of events anyway. And in their answers, we can see that Adam shifted the blame to Eve ("that woman you gave me…"), and Eve shifted the blame to Satan ("the serpent deceived me"). Satan had nowhere to point the finger, so he was silent.

When we sin, it is common for us to attempt to shift the blame. Adam and Eve felt naked and exposed after they sinned, and they pointed the finger away from themselves. We are their children; we share their inclinations to sin and the subsequent blame-shifting (Psalm 51:5, 58:3; Romans 3:9-18).

No one likes to have their sin struggles exposed, and some will attempt to place the blame for their involvement with sexual impurity in part or whole with their spouse, their parents, their circumstances, etc. Some will go as far as Adam did and blame God. Even the injured party will do this if they respond sinfully, but when we push fault onto another person, we are not thinking biblically or correctly.

Question 2: Have you or your spouse tried to shift blame for your personal sin onto each other? Please share.

_____

_____

_____

_____

Hearing accusations of: "You aren't pretty enough, thin enough, smart enough, sexy enough, available enough…and that's why I view pornography, etc." can be very painful. But we can comfort ourselves with the knowledge that God will not allow these sin-fueled accusations to go unchecked. If you have put your faith in Jesus as your Savior, then you are a child of God, and your Heavenly Father will come to your aid at the right time.

So, do not argue with your spouse if they hurl accusations at you (Proverbs 26:4) or if they attempt to shift blame to you or others. Arguing aggravates the situation further, and even worse, it pits you against your spouse, which is precisely what the devil wants. Don't fall for Satan's tricks. Hold your tongue and look to Jesus (Hebrews 12:1-3; 1 Peter 2:23).

Now that we know what not to do, let's return to our reading of Genesis 3 and see God's response to Adam and Eve's sin and blame-shifting. We will see that God determines the consequences of sin, but He also gives hope for their future.

> *"So, the Lord God said to the serpent, "Because you have done this, "Cursed are you above all livestock and all wild animals! You will crawl on your belly, and you will eat dust all the days of your life. And I will put enmity between you and the woman, and between your offspring and hers; he will crush your head, and you will strike his heel." To the woman, he said, "I will make your pains in childbearing very severe; with painful labor, you will give birth to children. Your desire will be for your husband, and he will rule over you." To Adam, he said, "Because you listened to your wife and ate fruit from the tree about which I commanded you, 'You must not eat from it,' "Cursed is the ground because of you; through painful toil, you will eat food from it all the days of your life. It will produce thorns and thistles for you, and you will eat the plants of the field. By the sweat of your brow, you will eat your food until you return to the ground since from it you were taken; for dust you are, and to dust, you will return." Adam named his wife Eve because she would become the mother of all the living. The Lord God made garments of skin for Adam and his wife and clothed them." Genesis 3:14-21*

Question 3: Please study Genesis 3 and list all the consequences you can find that God gave to Adam and Eve because of their sin:

_____

_____

_____

_____

These verses always bring tears to my eyes. Who of us hasn't experienced the consequences of our sin? Adam and Eve were surely devastated. But God does not leave them (or us) without hope. Read on for a message of hope which you can share with your spouse.

Question 4: According to Genesis 3:21, what did God do for Adam and Eve?
- ☐ He laughed at them
- ☐ He clothed them
- ☐ He ignored them

After Adam and Eve sinned, their eyes were opened, and they knew that they were naked (Genesis 3:7). Immediately, they attempted to cover themselves by sewing together fig leaves, but their efforts to cover themselves and hide from God were not successful.

Adam and Eve attempted to cover themselves and clothe their nakedness with real fig leaves, but we might also discern that the fig leaves are symbolic of 'works,' human efforts to cover themselves after their sin. But again, Genesis 3:21 teaches us that their efforts to conceal themselves did not work, as God clothed them with the skins of an animal instead.

Though the Scripture does not explicitly say God put to death an animal, in the context of the rest of Scripture we understand that to obtain the skins, God did indeed have to sacrifice an animal. God put to death a substitute for Adam and Eve.

And here we find application for our lives. When we sin, we feel naked and exposed. We want to hide, or we want to make ourselves right again by our own efforts. But God is good and merciful. He, Himself provides the solution to our sin problem. The cross of Jesus Christ shows that God *"devises means so that the banished one will not remain an outcast."* 2 Samuel 14:14

God did not leave Adam and Eve in their nakedness. He put to death a substitute, to both cover their sin and clothe them, so they would not have to remain estranged from God. God made this first sacrifice to illustrate His plans to save us all. This is the gospel in story form.

Adam and Eve sinned, and immediately they felt their nakedness and shame. First, they tried to cover it up with leaves, and they tried to shift the blame elsewhere. None of this worked to make themselves right with God. The New Testament makes it clear that this is true for us as well:

We cannot be right with God by our works; that is, the "fig leaves" of our efforts, but only through our Substitute, Jesus:

> *"For we ourselves were once foolish, disobedient, led astray, slaves to various passions and pleasures, passing our days in malice and envy, hated by others and hating one another. But when the goodness and loving kindness of God our Savior appeared, he saved us, not because of works done by us in righteousness, but according to his own mercy, by the washing of regeneration and renewal of the Holy Spirit, whom he poured out on us richly through Jesus Christ our Savior,"* Titus 3:3-6

Question 5: According to Titus 3:5, by what did God save us?
- ☐ By our own good works
- ☐ By being baptized in the church
- ☐ By the washing of regeneration and renewal of the Holy Spirit through Jesus

In Genesis 3, God demonstrated the Way of Salvation. He had the Plan that would succeed. God put to death an innocent animal and provided a covering for Adam and Eve.

Revelation 13:8 tells us that Jesus' death on the cross and subsequent resurrection was the plan of God the Father, Son and Spirit before the universe was created. By one man's disobedience (Adam), mankind was plunged into a life of sin; but by one man's (Jesus) act of obedience, we are redeemed (Romans 5:19). Because of Jesus, our situation is full of hope!

We feel the same shame and blame and nakedness that Adam and Eve felt. Our natural inclination is to say, "It is his fault." "It is her fault."

But Jesus reaches out His arms and says, "Blame me, Father. I will take on all the shame, nakedness, and guilt. I will receive all Your wrath. I will atone for the sins of my people. I will die so that they can be covered. I will pay for their sin."

Friend, fix your eyes on Jesus (Hebrews 12:2):

- See Him dying to take away your sin and that of your spouse.
- See Jesus suffering and pouring out His whole life so that you and your spouse might be forgiven, and your marriage might be saved.
- See Him rising again and ascending to the Father victorious (Hebrews 1:3).
- See Him interceding on your behalf, praying for you right now (Hebrews 7:25).

Don't get caught up in the blame-shifting trap of the devil. Instead, look to Jesus and be filled with the joy of your salvation and hope for your situation.

> **Question 6:** Does the gospel give you hope for your marriage? Please explain.

Why?

*W*elcome back, friend. It is good to see you pressing on in your course.

In lesson 12, we began a discussion about sin and blame. We saw from the Scriptures that our spouse's sin is not our fault, nor is our sin their fault. We also understood the folly of blame-shifting, and we prepared ourselves with a gospel response to any blame-shifting that might happen. In the end, we rejoiced in our Savior Who took the blame for us all.

Today, we are going to address the issue of why our spouse struggles with sexual impurity more directly. It is an important topic for us to consider because the world is going to tell us that our spouse is an "addict" and unable to change. We need to know that as children of the Living God, we are different. In Christ, we are new creations filled with the Holy Spirit and where the Spirit of the Lord is there is freedom (2 Corinthians 3:17).

Let's begin with the fundamental question: why do we sin?

The Scriptures tell us that we sin because we live in bodies of flesh in a fallen world. Paul wrote in Romans 5:12, *"Therefore, just as sin came into the world through one man, and death through sin, and so death spread to all men because all sinned."* When Adam and Eve sinned, they birthed a heritage of sin and death for us all. From birth, we are sinful (Psalm 58:3); this is the condition of all mankind (Job 15:14; Ephesians 2:3).

The world will tell you that your spouse is a sex addict. The world blames immoral behavior on bad parenting, unbalanced brain chemistry, sexual molestation during childhood, or a myriad of other things. The problem with this type of thinking is that it is hopeless. There is no cure for our past or our "bad" parents. I do not mean to minimize anyone's pain, or the sins committed against us in childhood, but we cannot change those things. It is futile to point to those events as the reason for our current actions.

Additionally, this type of worldly reasoning is not only inaccurate but also inconsistent. Many people have had horrible childhood experiences but "against all the odds" gone on to live healthy, productive lives. Conversely, some come from idyllic childhoods who grow up to live gross lives of sin and debauchery.

> **Question 1:** Have you struggled with trying to understand the reasons why your spouse involved themselves with sexual sin? Please share.
>
> _____
>
> _____
>
> _____
>
> _____

Friend, your spouse did not involve themselves with sexual sin because you are not enough or because of some irreversible brokenness in their life. Sexual sin is a common struggle and while there are many factors that might foster or encourage an immoral mindset, the heart of the matter is that we are all born with a propensity to sin. This is the primary reason why your spouse became involved with sexual impurity.

The good news is that God did not abandon us in our sin; He devised a way for us to be set free from the power of sin. Jesus' obedience to death on the cross secured our forgiveness from sin and our freedom from its power!

We are all born dead in our sins (Ephesians 2:1), but God so loved the world that He sent His one and only Son Jesus to enter into our humanity (John 3:16), to become sin for us (2 Corinthians 5:21), to pay the penalty for our transgressions (1 Peter 2:24), to absorb the just wrath of God in our place (Romans 3:25) so that we might be righteous (Romans 5:19) in God's sight and accepted by the Father (Ephesians 1:6).

Question 2: What is it that broke the power of sin in the lives of those who believe in Jesus?

☐ The Ten Commandments

☐ Hours of Therapy

☐ Jesus' death on the cross and His victorious resurrection

But as we have all experienced, we will, at times, find ourselves (or our spouse) caught in sin traps (Galatians 6:1). Let us continue in our study of the Word to discover why we Christians, at times sink beneath the waves of temptation.

Please read Matthew 14:24-33, *"but the boat by this time was a long way from the land, beaten by the waves, for the wind was against them. And in the fourth watch of the night, he came to them, walking on the sea. But when the disciples saw him walking on the sea, they were terrified, and said, "It is a ghost!" and they cried out in fear. But immediately Jesus spoke to them, saying, "Take heart; it is I. Do not be afraid." And Peter answered him, "Lord, if it is you, command me to come to you on the water." He said, "Come." So, Peter got out of the boat and walked on the water and came to Jesus. But when he saw the wind, he was afraid, and beginning to sink he cried out, "Lord, save me." (Matthew 14:24-30)*

After feeding the five thousand, Jesus sent his disciples on ahead of him in the boat. But the disciples' journey across the sea was not an easy one. In our text, we see them working against the wind and caught up in a storm when Jesus comes walking out to them. At first, they are all terrified, but then Jesus speaks to them words of peace and encouragement. And Peter asks to walk out to Jesus on the water.

> **Question 3:** At Jesus' call to come, Peter walked on the water towards Jesus. According to verse 30, when did Peter begin to sink? Fill in the blank. *"But when he _____the _____, he was _____, and beginning to _____..."*

When Peter took his eyes off Jesus and began to focus on the wind and the waves, he began to sink.

Dear friend, this is not merely a story about Peter sinking in a storm, it is a lesson for us all.

When we take our eyes off Jesus, we will get into trouble.
When we focus on our circumstances, ourselves, our fleshly
desires, anything other than our Savior, we will sink.

Our believing spouse became ensnared in sexual impurity because they took their eyes off Jesus. What distracted them is not uncommon, but it will be unique to each person. Maybe it is a stressful job, a sick child, an immoral woman or man, boredom, guilt, frustration, etc. The devil has countless "winds and waves" to swirl around God's people, but his goal is always the same: to kill, steal, and destroy (John 10:10).

> **Question 4:** What are some things which have distracted you or your spouse from Jesus? Please share.
>
> _____
>
> _____
>
> _____
>
> _____

There are many distractions in this life, but in Christ, we can overcome them. Let's look again at our text in Matthew 14 and find the solution for sinking.

> *Peter got out of the boat and walked on the water and came to Jesus. But when he saw the wind, he was afraid, and beginning to sink he cried out, "Lord, save me." Jesus immediately reached out his hand and took hold of him, saying to him, "O you of little faith, why did you doubt?" (Matthew 14:29-31).*

> **Question 5:** According to Matthew 14:30, what did Peter do when he began to sink?
> - ☐ He asked Phillip to throw him a life preserver.
> - ☐ He swam back to the boat
> - ☐ He cried out, "Lord, save me."

Peter cried out, *"Lord, save me."* It seems so simple, doesn't it? And in many ways, it is. When we find ourselves sinking in any situation, we need only call out to Jesus. He is mighty to save.

At Peter's cry for help, Jesus immediately reached out, took hold of Peter and brought him to safety within the boat. Then Jesus raises the same question to Peter that we are addressing in this lesson, "Why?"

Jesus asked Peter, *"Why did you doubt?"* not because Jesus didn't know the answer, but rather Jesus questioned Peter in love to teach Peter a vital truth: He wanted Peter to see that when we lose our focus on Christ, we doubt and fear, and sink.

All sin struggles for us Christians stem from losing focus on Jesus, which leads to doubting God. And the solution is always to look to and call out to Jesus. When we do, we will discover that He has us too; He raises us and saves us. The solution to our doubting is to put our eyes back on Jesus where they belong.

Now notice what happened when Jesus reached out for Peter and took him safely back to the boat.

And when they got into the boat, the wind ceased. And those in the boat worshiped him, saying, "Truly you are the Son of God." (Matthew 14:32-33) The wind ceased; the storm stopped in the presence of Jesus!

Dear friend, when we find ourselves in a storm, we must cry out to Jesus, lift our eyes to Jesus and point others (husband, children, friends, everyone) to Jesus! Because as long as our eyes are on Jesus, we will be able to "walk" through the storm. And at the proper time, He will cause the storm to cease.

As we conclude our study today, let's note one more thing from our text.

Question 6: According to verse 33, what did the disciples do
after the storm stopped?
   ☐ They laughed.
   ☐ They worshipped.
   ☐ They slept.

The right response to the work of our Savior Jesus is always to worship. He is the Son of God. He is the One who can calm the storm in our hearts and minds. He is the One who is mighty to save. He is the Lamb who was worthy to be slain—the perfect, spotless One who gave His life to save us.

We started this lesson seeking to understand the why of sexual sin, but we are ending it worshipping the One who is ready and able to reach into the waves of sexual sin and save anyone who calls for help.

If you are struggling today with sin of any kind, call out to Jesus; He is ready to save. I also encourage you to speak words of life and hope to your spouse today—tell him that there is hope for true and lasting freedom in Jesus. Don't doubt; trust in God's unfailing love and rejoice in His salvation (Psalm 13:5).

Question 7: Are you looking to Jesus to save and sustain you in your current circumstances? Please share.

_____

_____

_____

_____

Speaking the Gospel in Words of Life

*H*ello, friend, and welcome back to the A United Front course.

We ended day 13 with an encouragement to speak "words of life" to your spouse, and in this lesson, we study what it means to speak words of life.

Words are powerful. *"Death and life are in the power of the tongue"* (Proverbs 18:21), and as Christians, we are called only to speak that which builds up and gives grace.

> **Question 1:** According to Ephesians 4:29, what should characterize your conversation? Fill in the blank, *"Let _____ _____ talk come out of your mouths, but _____ such as is _____ for _____ _____, as fits the occasion, that it may _____ _____ to those who hear."*

Habitual sin in a marriage often evokes unkind words. In pain, we might lash out with unkind words. In anger, we might speak destructively and tear down our spouse with our words (Proverbs 14:1). It is a common sin struggle. But God is merciful. We can repent of corrupting talk, and God's grace can teach us a new way of communicating (Proverbs 12:18).

We can learn to build up others with our words, but we must first address a deeper issue. Jesus explained it to His disciples this way, *"The good person out of the good treasure of his heart produces good, and the evil person out of his evil treasure produces evil, for out of the abundance of the heart his mouth speaks." (Luke 6:45)*

Question 2: According to Luke 6:45, our mouths speak from the abundance of what is in our _____?

- ☐ Hands
- ☐ Heart
- ☐ Lungs

Whatever is in our hearts will eventually come out of our mouths. This truth is never more evident than when adversity comes.

If we have self-righteousness in our hearts, then our words will be harsh and judgmental towards those who sin against us. Conversely, if the love of Jesus is in our hearts, then our speech will be humble and kind even in the face of offense.

Question 3: Think about the things you have said to your spouse lately, what does what you have said reveal about what is in your heart? Please share.

_____

_____

_____

_____

I am grieved to remember how the evils of anger, jealousy, bitterness, and fear once filled my heart, and even more to know that those evils came out of my mouth as wounding words.

So, what are we to do if we find that evil is in our hearts and not good? We know we need to change, but how? There is a solution to this problem, and we can see it illustrated in the Old Testament. Please read with me:

> *"Elisha returned to Gilgal and there was a famine in that region. While the company of the prophets was meeting with him, he said to his servant, "Put on the large pot and cook some stew for these prophets." One of them went out into the fields to gather herbs and found a wild vine and picked as many of its gourds as his garment could hold. When he returned, he cut them up into the*

pot of stew, though no one knew what they were. The stew was poured out for the men, but as they began to eat it, they cried out, "Man of God, there is death in the pot!" And they could not eat it. Elisha said, "Get some flour." He put it into the pot and said, "Serve it to the people to eat." And there was nothing harmful in the pot." 2 Kings 4:38-41 (NIV)

In 2 Kings 4, we read of Elisha and a large company of prophets who were meeting together. There was a famine in the land, scavenging for food was necessary, but this time there was a problem. They made stew, but the stew contained poisonous gourds, and when they tasted it, they experienced the bitterness of the "death in the pot."

> **Question 4:** According to 2 Kings 4: 41, what did Elisha do to solve the problem?
> ☐ He strained the stew
> ☐ He picked out all the poisonous gourds
> ☐ He added flour

Elisha did not go on a mission to pull out all the poisonous gourds in the stew—the poison had permeated the entire pot. Instead, Elisha put flour into the pot and miraculously the stew became edible. Possibly the flour drew to itself all the poison in the pot and left nutritionally healthy stew.

We know that we can find application for our lives in this story because Jesus told his disciples on the road to Emmaus that the Old Testament Scriptures spoke about Him (Luke 24:25-27) and this story is no exception.

Think of how God sent His Son right into the midst of this poisonous world. He came from the glories of heaven to this "pot of death" in which we live, and He went to the cross to deal with our sin problem. And here is where God performed the miracle!

As Jesus hung on the cross, He drew to Himself all our sin, all the evil poison of our sinful hearts—past, present, and future. He *"became sin for us…"* (2 Corinthians 5:21a).

And what was the result? He purified us! *"…that we might become the righteousness of God in Him" (2 Corinthians 5:21b).* There is no more "death in the pot" for those who believe in Jesus. Jesus took our death and gave us life eternal! He absorbed all the evil and then replaced it with His love (Romans 5:5).

Now with our thoughts centered in the gospel, let's consider the miracle of the transformed stew again, and see if we can apply it to the issue of our hearts and how they affect our speech.

Our hearts are like the pot, aren't they? Whatever we put in our heart is what will pour out of our mouths when we speak.

Sadly, there are times when you might unwittingly take poison into your heart. Maybe it is through listening to worldly counsel, or perhaps it enters when you dwell on negative thoughts about your spouse. You can't pick the poison out, but you can neutralize the poison by adding in the gospel of Jesus. As you do, Jesus' love, which is poured into your heart by His Holy Spirit (Romans 5:5) will cause beautiful words of life to flow freely from you to those around you.

> **Question 5:** How can you take in more of the gospel of Jesus today? Please share.
>
> _____
>
> _____
>
> _____
>
> _____

"Finally, brothers, whatever is true, whatever is honorable, whatever is just, whatever is pure, whatever is lovely, whatever is commendable, if there is any excellence, if there is anything worthy of praise, think about these things." Philippians 4:8

Here we learn that we are to think about what is true, honorable, just, pure, lovely, commendable, excellent and praiseworthy and Scripture teaches us that Jesus is all of these:

- **Jesus is true:** Jesus said to him, "I am the way, and the truth, and the life. No one comes to the Father except through me." John 14:6
- **Jesus is honorable:** "Jesus has been found worthy of greater honor than Moses, just as the builder of a house has greater honor than the house itself." Hebrews 3:3 NIV
- **Jesus is just:** "…you are in Christ Jesus, who became to us wisdom from God, righteousness and sanctification and redemption, so that, as it is written, "Let the one who boasts, boast in the Lord." 1 Corinthians 1:30-31
- **Jesus is pure:** "And everyone who thus hopes in him purifies himself as he is pure". 1 John 3:3
- **Jesus is lovely:** "he is altogether lovely." Song of Solomon 5:16 NIV
- **Jesus is commendable:** "For when he received honor and glory from God the Father, and the voice was borne to him by the Majestic Glory, "This is my beloved Son, with whom I am well pleased," 2 Peter 1:17
- **Jesus is excellent:** "O Lord, our Lord, how excellent is thy name in all the earth!" Psalm 8:1 KJV
- **Jesus is worthy of praise:** "…Worthy is the Lamb who was slain, to receive power and wealth and wisdom and might and honor and glory and blessing! And I heard every creature in heaven and on earth and under the earth and in the sea, and all that is in them, saying, "To him who sits on the throne and to the Lamb be blessing and honor and glory and might forever and ever!" Revelation 5:11-13

Oh, friend, we need to meditate on Jesus and His gospel. By His death and resurrection, Jesus has secured the purifying miracle that we need for our heart.

Do you find yourself struggling with fears, doubts, anger or disappointment? Do you find mean, ugly or evil words pouring out of your mouth when you are distressed?

Think of Jesus and let His death and resurrection fill your heart and mind, and your troublesome thoughts will be crowded out by all the good, true and excellent thoughts of the One who died and rose again to save and sanctify you.

Ask Jesus, the Word of God made flesh, to transform your words so that you speak life and not death. He is faithful; He will do it (1 Thessalonians 5:24).

Question 6: Write out some pure and lovely thoughts that you will think about today so that your heart will be centered in the gospel of Jesus.

_____

_____

_____

_____

As your heart is encouraged by the gospel, you will want to share these words of life with your spouse.

For example:

- If your spouse expresses that their sin is too great and that God cannot forgive them, encourage them with the truth of the gospel: our God is mighty to save (Isa 63:1)! There is no sin so great that it cannot be forgiven (Psalm 51). "Through him, everyone who believes is set free from every sin, a justification you were not able to obtain under the law of Moses" (Acts 13:39).
- If your spouse doesn't believe that they can break free of their sin struggle, encourage them with the gospel: Jesus overcame death and hell, and if we believe in Him His Spirit lives within us; and if Christ's Spirit is in us then we can overcome our flesh (Romans 8:7-38) by looking to and fixing our eyes on Jesus (Hebrews 12:1-3).

Question 7: How can you speak words of life (the gospel) to your spouse today? Think through what specific words you might use and write them here.

_____

_____

_____

_____

I pray that you will not only speak words of life to your spouse but also to your own heart, dear friend. We need the good news of hope found at the cross, abundant life through Jesus' death (John 10:10), and eternal life through Jesus' sacrifice (John 3:16).

Exchanging Old for New at the Cross

*H*ello, friend, and welcome back!

In lesson 14, we learned from Ephesians 4:29, the importance of speaking words that build up and give grace to those around us. We learned that our words flow out of what is in our hearts and understood that if we want to transform our speech, we must fill our hearts with the gospel truth of Jesus who is pure and lovely. Finally, we learned that we could speak words of life to our spouse by centering our conversation in the gospel.

Gospel-centered speech is loving, kind, compassionate, hope-filled, and restoring just as Christ's death on the cross was an act of love, kindness, and compassion which provided hope to a lost and dying world and restored us to a right relationship with the Father. But this manner of speaking does not come naturally to anyone; it is a supernatural way of communicating.

By nature, we all respond to our circumstances according to the flesh. When someone sins against us, perhaps we say mean things, give the cold shoulder, deliver dirty looks, bang pots, or withhold affection; this is how the flesh responds to offenses. But as followers of Christ, we are called to walk in the gracious Spirit of Jesus. So, for these next several lessons, we will focus on identifying what needs to change and how to make the change.

We will study the biblical principle of putting off sinful actions and responses and putting on gospel-centered actions and reactions. Jesus put off His righteousness and put on our sin so that we might be made right with God. In response, we must put off our sinful ways and put on His righteousness.

Please read Ephesians 4:17-24 and answer the questions that follow:

"Now this I say and testify in the Lord, that you must no longer walk as the Gentiles do, in the futility of their minds. They are darkened in their understanding, alienated from the life of God because of the ignorance that is in them, due to their hardness of heart. They have become callous and have given themselves up to sensuality, greedy to practice every kind of impurity. But that is not the way you learned Christ!—assuming that you have heard about him and were taught in him, as the truth is in Jesus, to put off your old self, which belongs to your former manner of life and is corrupt through deceitful desires, and to be renewed in the spirit of your minds, and to put on the new self, created after the likeness of God in true righteousness and holiness."

Writing to the Church in Ephesus, Paul describes the Gentiles or unbelievers as hard-hearted, dark-minded, ignorant, separated from God living futile lives of impurity. And it is into this unbelieving way that we are all born. And the sad part is that even after we come to faith and new life in Christ, we might still act or live like unbelievers.

When I first found out about my husband's sin, I reacted to the news as an unbeliever with anger and frustration. I responded to my husband's sin as a woman of fear, not faith. I was self-centered, devoid of grace and mercy.

Question 1: What about you? Can you remember a time when you lived or acted in a way that an unbeliever might? Please share.

_____

_____

_____

Clearly, the Church at Ephesus was struggling in this area too because Paul writes, "You must no longer walk as the Gentiles...that's not the way you learned Christ!"

Question 2: According to Ephesians 4:22-24, what are we to do?

- ☐ Give vent to our anger about our spouse's impurity and make them feel the pain of their sin.
- ☐ Shame our spouses so that they would learn to change.
- ☐ Put off our old selves, be renewed in our minds and put on our new selves.

By His death, Christ made a new and living way for us (Hebrews 10:20) for us to be right with the Father and with one another. So, if we are in Christ, then we have the power to live differently, and we should live differently.

For a long time, I did not understand how this worked. For example, as a child, I was known for being very animated. "Jody talks too much in class" was the most commonly written remark on my report cards. And for years, I believed that I would always be outspoken and dominating. But since I've come to know more of Jesus, I've learned that change is possible. By God's grace, I am learning to live in gentleness, quietness, and humility.

As Christians, we are not bound by our personalities, our heritage, our families, our denomination, or anything else. You are not obliged to have a hot temper, overeat, act rudely or any other improper thing just because your family is Polish, Dutch, Irish, German, Mexican, Italian, French, Russian, African, etc. Your hair color and height do not determine who you are; your body is just a tent housing the real you. We must understand and embrace the truth that is in Christ: we have a new identity, family, and life (Romans 6, Matthew 12: 48-50, Acts 5:20)!

Sometimes it is hard to know what needs to change. Read Colossians 3:5-9 for some insight about what is of the "old self" and what we should reject as children of God.

Colossians 3 5-9 "Put to death therefore what is earthly in you: sexual immorality, impurity, passion, evil desire, and covetousness, which is idolatry. On account of these, the wrath of God is coming. In these, you too once walked, when you were living in them. But now you must put them all away: anger, wrath, malice, slander, and obscene talk from your mouth. Do not lie to one another, seeing that you have put off the old self with its practices..."

The temptation at this point might be to think of others like your spouse, children, friends, or family, and how they need to change. But you must focus on your own heart and think about what you need to change.

God has enabled me to put off habitual sins such as fear, lying, selfishness, pride, sinful anger, gossip, slander, anxiety, malice, covetousness, a judgmental spirit, and more. I have not attained, but by God's grace and through the love of Jesus, the gospel is transforming me. I am learning to leave the old ways behind and embrace the new and living way; the way I learn in Jesus.

Question 3: Please share what "earthly" things you want to "put to death" in your life.

_____

_____

_____

_____

Putting off is only the first part. Jesus did not only take off His royal robes of righteousness; he also went on to become sin for us so that we might become the righteousness of God (2 Corinthians 5:21). At the cross, there was a great exchange: Christ took your sin and gave you His righteousness.

There must be an exchange in our lives as well. We cannot simply turn away from the behavior we know to be wrong because to do so is to deny the power of the gospel. We must go on to receive from Christ the new way of life that He has for us. As Ephesians 4 says, we must *"put on"* the new self. We can read a fuller picture of what this is like in Colossians 3:12-17:

> *"Put on then, as God's chosen ones, holy and beloved, compassionate hearts, kindness, humility, meekness, and patience, bearing with one another and, if one has a complaint against another, forgiving each other; as the Lord has forgiven you, so you also must forgive. And above all these put on love, which binds everything together in perfect harmony."*

Question 4: According to Colossians 3:12-14, what are we to put on as God's chosen ones. Fill in the blank. *"Put on then, as God's chosen ones, holy and beloved, _____ hearts, _____, _____, _____, and _____, bearing with one another and, if one has a complaint against another, _____ each other; as the Lord has forgiven you, so you also must forgive. And above all these put on _____, which binds everything together in perfect harmony."*

As you read through Colossians 3:12-14, did you notice that these are all attributes of Christ? Jesus is holy, beloved, compassionate, kind, humble, meek, patient, long-suffering, forgiving, and loving! Our goal is to be transformed from our old way of life into His...to be like Jesus.

It is imperative that we always remember Christ is our aim. We are not seeking to merely change behaviors; we want to be transformed into the image of our Lord through grace. And as we keep our eyes on Christ, think about His cross, consult Him in everything, we will find that this transformation happens from the inside out (2 Corinthians 3:18).

In our next lesson, we will continue our study of putting on our new life; I believe you'll find it helpful. For now, I want to leave you with these encouraging words:

- Jesus loves you and your husband (1 John 3:16).
- Jesus knows the sorrows, confusion, unrest and questions of your life; and He has good news for you (Luke 4:18-21).
- Jesus offers joy in exchange for your sorrow (Jeremiah 31).
- Jesus gives wisdom in exchange for your perplexed mind (James 1:5).
- Jesus brings to you peace in exchange for your worry (Philippians 4:7).
- Jesus is the answer to all of your questions (John 14:6).
- Jesus is the One you are seeking; and if you seek Him, you will find Him (Matthew 7:7-8).

You need not despair, accept the status quo, or resign yourself to endure your situation. In Christ, change is possible! Do not believe the lies of this world, such as "once an addict always an addict." Remember 1 Corinthians 6:11, *"And such **were** some of you. But you were washed, you were sanctified, you were justi-fied in the name of the Lord Jesus Christ and by the Spirit of our God."* There is hope for change through the gospel of Jesus Christ.

Question 5: What are your final thoughts about this lesson? Please share.

_____

_____

_____

_____

Compassionate Hearts
From the Cross

*H*ello and welcome back to the A United Front course.

In Lesson 15, we learned that through His death and resurrection, Christ made a new and living way for us. To walk in His way, we must put off our old way of life (the actions of an unbeliever). We made a list of "old ways" we want to put off which included things such as malice, dominance, disrespect, sinful anger, revenge, self-pity, impurity, gossip, rebellion, pride, and deceit. And we understood from Ephesians 4 and Colossians 3 that Christ took away our filthy rags and gave us gleaming robes of righteousness. As dearly loved and chosen children, we must embrace Him, rejoice in our new "clothes" and learn Christ's way of living.

By way of review, please read Colossians 3:12-17. We will be studying this passage in detail over the coming lessons. Let's begin with verse 12:

> *Put on then, as God's chosen ones, holy and beloved, compassionate hearts, kindness, humility, meekness, and patience,*

Question 1: According to Colossians 3:12, what are we to "put on" first?
- ☐ Generous Hands
- ☐ Compassionate Hearts
- ☐ Perfect Behavior

First, we are told to put on a compassionate heart. Having a compassionate heart might sound simple at first consideration, but the concept is a weighty one. The original Greek words translate to *"bowels of mercies,"* communicating that this is mercy flowing from the very core of our being—deep and sacrificial compassion.

This type of compassion sees another's plight and, moved by love, takes action to help. These same words are used to describe the compassion and mercy that God had on us when He gave His Son Jesus to die in our place (Luke 1:78).

Let's pause and consider the mercy and compassion of our God as this will help us to understand the compassionate heart we are to seek.

Think of it, friend, you were born dead in your sins, without hope and separated from God; but God, who is rich in mercy, sent His perfect Son to die in your place. Jesus bore the guilt of your sin to give you eternal life. He then rose from the dead, proof that God accepted His sacrifice, to justify you before the Father. *"He was delivered over to death for our sins and was raised to life for our justification." Romans 4:25 (NIV)*

Yes, God had compassion on us and took action to help us; because of His compassionate heart toward us, we benefitted though we did not deserve it, and as His children, we can now extend genuine compassion to others.

> **Question 2:** Considering God's compassionate heart toward you, do you have a compassionate heart toward your spouse? Why or why not?
>
> _____
>
> _____
>
> _____
>
> _____

My heart aches as I consider how I initially lacked compassion for my husband. I was the opposite of a compassionate heart; I had an angry and vengeful spirit. His betrayal hurt me, and I wanted him to suffer for it. I wanted compassion for me, not him. My initial thinking was that if I could make the experience terrible enough for my husband, then he would never want to sin against me again in this way. Sadly, I was living in the old ways—responding in the flesh— and the result of my actions was proof of it.

My husband did feel terrible for his sins against me, but because he felt ashamed and guilt-ridden around me, he no longer wanted to spend time with me. Our marriage problems were compounded by my responding according to the old way of the flesh.

Once I learned the new way of the gospel, the way of Christ and His compassionate heart, things began to change for the good:

- I began to show compassion for my husband as a sister in Christ who has her own sin struggles. I began to show him that I was his compassionate partner in our marriage by doing whatever it took to help him to overcome the world, the flesh, and the devil.
- My husband began to see me as a friend; he wanted to unite with me.
- Our marriage grew stronger as God's compassion reigned in our hearts and lives.

If you need to cultivate a compassionate heart toward your spouse, then know that we can indeed become compassionate people, not by our own efforts to change, but by the power of the Holy Spirit who works in us (Philippians 2:13).

Even if you feel your heart is as cold as ice toward your husband, God can thaw you out. How does He do this? With His immeasurable and relentless love and compassion. We must *receive* compassion and comfort from God from the supply of His unmerited grace to us before we can *give* it to our spouses so that it's from the *overflow* of His compassion in our lives that we can be compassionate to our spouses:

> *"Praise be to the God and Father of our Lord Jesus Christ, the Father of compassion and the God of all comfort, who comforts us in all our troubles so that we can comfort those in any trouble with the comfort we ourselves have received from God. For just as the sufferings of Christ flow over into our lives, so also through Christ our comfort overflows." 2 Corinthians 1:3-5 (NIV)*

As we consider how we can begin to put on a compassionate heart, let's look to 2 Corinthians 3:18, *"And we all, with unveiled face, beholding the glory of the Lord, are being transformed into the same image from one degree of glory to another. For this comes from the Lord who is the Spirit."*

Question 3: According to 2 Corinthians 3:18, what happens as we behold the glory of the Lord:

☐ We are transformed into the image of Christ.
☐ We are transported to another world.
☐ We are blinded by the light.

As we behold the glory of the Lord we are transformed; we are changed into the same image, by degrees. But you might ask, what is the glory of the Lord? What exactly am I to behold? Hebrews 1 explains this for us:

"Long ago, at many times and in many ways, God spoke to our fathers by the prophets, but in these last days he has spoken to us by his Son, whom he appointed the heir of all things, through whom also he created the world. He is the radiance of the glory of God and the exact imprint of his nature, and he upholds the universe by the word of his power. After making purification for sins, he sat down at the right hand of the Majesty on high…" Hebrews 1:1-3

Question 4: According to Hebrews 1:3, Who is the glory of God?

☐ Moses
☐ Michael the Archangel
☐ Jesus Christ

Christ is the Son through whom God has spoken. Jesus is the glory of God. Jesus is the one we must look to, behold, fix our eyes upon if we want to be changed.

Question 5: How are you "beholding" Christ daily? Please share.

_____

_____

_____

My friend Stacy explained the process this way: "My sons watched a movie about Daniel Boone, and immediately they began to play as if they were Daniel Boone. They pretended to stalk bears in the woods, chop down trees, build log cabins and explore new lands. Their lives reflected what they had seen in Daniel Boone. It is the same for us as well. As we fix our eyes on Christ and consider how He lived and died then we, too, will live and even die differently. We will learn to live like Jesus by "beholding" Him."

Indeed, we will be changed by looking to Jesus. And, dear friend, you must specifically look to the death and resurrection of Jesus. Remember Hebrews 12:1-2, *"looking to Jesus, the founder and perfecter of our faith, who for the joy that was set before him endured the cross, despising the shame, and is seated at the right hand of the throne of God. Consider him who endured from sinners such hostility against himself, so that you may not grow weary or fainthearted."*

You'll notice that we are to look to Jesus who endured the cross—our sin, our shame, the wrath of God, the hostility of us sinners—to save us. As we consider all that Christ has accomplished on our behalf, as we gaze at Him—beholding and considering the Lamb that takes away the sin of the world—as we see the compassionate heart of God displayed so vividly, we cannot help but be affected and changed. As we view the death and resurrection of Jesus, over and over, we are seeing the glory of the Lord.

Question 6: How does God's compassion affect your heart, as you look at the cross? Please explain.

I hope your heart is full to overflowing today as you have considered God's compassion toward you. I pray that His love inspires compassion in your own heart and that all whom you encounter will know that you have been with Jesus (Acts 4:13).

The compassion of Christ in my heart enabled me to show compassion to my husband by being empathetic with him in his struggle against the habitual sins that had trapped him. I began to see my husband not as someone who was out to hurt me or whose sins were malicious, but rather as a man who was caught in a trap of the devil. I saw him as one who needed my help to overcome.

So, instead of pushing my husband away, I *"put on"* compassion and drew my husband close to me in various ways such as: listening to him when he was struggling, helping him to prepare for his job, taking time throughout the day to check in with him to see if I could assist him in some way, making time to be with him as his wife, lover, and friend, and praying with him.

Question 7: How can you show compassion toward your spouse today?

_____

_____

_____

_____

Tomorrow, we will move on to consider more of the new way of gospel living.

Gospel-Centered Kindness

*H*ello and welcome back to the A United Front course. I hope that you are finding hope for your heart and help for your marriage as you study through the course lessons.

We are studying our way through the list of attributes given in Colossian 3 as a way of learning how to be a united front with our spouse. We began by learning what it means to put on a compassionate heart. We saw the compassionate heart of God displayed in the giving of His one and only Son, Jesus, to die as our atoning sacrifice. We saw the compassionate heart of Christ, who gave His very life's blood to secure our eternal salvation. We understood that to put on a compassionate heart requires sacrifice.

Our hearts are not naturally compassionate, especially when we are hurting. Our old way of life seeks to wound and shame the one who has offended us. However, in Christ, we are new creations (2 Corinthians 5:17). In Christ, we can respond to the sins of others in a compassionate way that empathizes with our offender and is willing to suffer loss to help them find freedom in the gospel.

Now, let us read Colossians 3:12-13 and continue in our pursuit of understanding the way that Christ teaches:

> *"Put on then, as God's chosen ones, holy and beloved, compassionate hearts, kindness, humility, meekness, and patience, bearing with one another and, if one has a complaint against another, forgiving each other; as the Lord has forgiven you, so you also must forgive."* (Colossians 3:12-13)

Question 1: According to Colossians 3, after a compassionate heart, what are we to put on as God's chosen ones?

☐ Power

☐ Fortitude

☐ Kindness

The act of being kind is something we often take for granted; and yet, it is probably one of the first things to go when we are angry or wounded. I had a wife once tell me that she wouldn't give her husband a drop of water even if he were dying of thirst. Her anger over her husband's sin of infidelity had driven out even the most rudimentary measure of kindness from her heart; but that type of thinking is of the flesh—the old way of life.

For many years now, there has been a concept circulating called "Random Acts of Kindness." The idea is to do acts of kindness randomly with the hopes that it will encourage others to do the same and thus make the world a better place. And while the idea is lovely, gospel kindness is much greater. The kindness of God is very intentional and purposeful. Being kind to strangers is easy—even an unbeliever can do it—but God calls us to a focused and sacrificial kindness that is supernatural and empowered by the Holy Spirit. As Luke 6:35 says, God *"is kind to the ungrateful and the evil."*

To understand the type of kindness we are talking about, let's consider God's actions toward the nation of Israel in Ezra 9:9, *"Though we are slaves, our God has not deserted us in our bondage. He has shown us kindness in the sight of the kings of Persia: He has granted us new life to rebuild the house of our God and repair its ruins, and he has given us a wall of protection in Judah and Jerusalem." (NIV)*

Question 2: In what condition were the people of Israel when God showed kindness to them?

☐ They were working hard and living well.

☐ They were in bondage and slavery.

☐ They were happy and free.

The people of Israel were in captivity and slaves when God showed kindness to them. But we shouldn't think of them as innocent slaves. Ezra is a book about the completion of the second temple and the return of God's people to Jerusalem after their exile. God had exiled the Israelites because they had abandoned the one true God and had begun worshiping the idols of the surrounding pagan nations. God gave them over to enslavement by those heathen nations to give them a physical representation of what had already occurred in their hearts.

Sound familiar? When our spouse abandoned us for impurity, they essentially entered into idolatry: the worship of self and sexual pleasure. It is wickedness, and God will not allow it to go unchecked. God always disciplines those He loves (Hebrews 12:6). But even in His discipline of His children, God is kind. Indeed, it is the kindness of God that leads us to repentance (Romans 2:4).

> **Question 3:** According to Ezra 9:9, what did God grant the people of Israel new life to do? Fill in the blank. "*He has granted us _____ _____ to rebuild the house of our God and _____ its _____...*"

God granted the people a new life to rebuild and repair. Dear friend, God is kind and generous; He granted slaves new life to restore and rebuild. And as Christ-followers, we want to display this same supernatural kindness toward our spouse, even while they are captivity or if they are ungrateful.

We must make room for restoration and healing. If we are always holding our spouse's sin over them, then there will be no healing, no new life, no restoration for them or us.

> **Question 4:** Have you been kind and made room for restoration in your marriage? Please share.

God not only dealt with the Israelites in kindness, but He has dealt with us this way too. Titus put it this way, *"For we ourselves were once foolish, disobedient, led astray, slaves to various passions and pleasures, passing our days in malice and envy, hated by others and hating one another. But when the goodness and loving kindness of God our Savior appeared, he saved us, not because of works done by us in righteousness, but according to his own mercy, by the washing of regeneration and renewal of the Holy Spirit, whom he poured out on us richly through Jesus Christ our Savior,"* (Titus 3:3-6)

We were foolish, disobedient, led astray, slaves to our various passions, malicious, envious, hated, and hating. These might be terms you associate with your spouse right now, but the reality is that we were all once this way.

I can remember a time when I acted hateful towards my husband. I lashed out at him, saying true but unkind and spiteful words. As soon as the words left my mouth, I felt Jesus' Holy Spirit reminding me of the cross of Christ. It was as if God said, "Was I mean to you? Did I throw your sin in your face? No, in kindness, I provided a way for your restoration."

As I considered my sin of unkindness, I wanted to blame my husband. After all, if he hadn't been immoral, I wouldn't have had a reason to be unkind; but, in time, God showed me that my husband's sins against me were not the cause of my sin struggles (Luke 6:45).

Walking this journey towards purity with my husband was humbling for me. I used to think I was a pretty good Christian, but God used the trauma of my husband's unfaithfulness to reveal the sins hidden in my own heart. And while it was a painful process, it was also a time of intense spiritual growth. I drew near to the Lord in desperation, seeking forgiveness and sustaining grace so that I might learn more of the way of Christ and how to be a true helper to my husband. God is faithful; He has changed me and continues to do so by His grace. He will do the same for you as well if you ask Him.

Question 5: Do you need to confess your lack of kindness toward your husband to God? Write out your prayer or share your thoughts here:

_____

_____

_____

_____

Confessing your lack of kindness to God is the first step, but you must also confess this sin to your spouse. Confessing to your spouse might seem awkward. You might think: what is unkindness compared with immorality? But I would encourage you to abandon any thoughts that your sin struggles aren't as bad as your spouse's, or that you don't need to confess anything until your spouse does. If you have been unkind to your spouse, seek the Lord for grace and go to your spouse and say something like this:

(spouse's name), I want to ask your forgiveness. God has shown me that I was unkind to you when I (fill in the blank); will you forgive me?

Don't worry about how your spouse responds. Remember you aren't asking for forgiveness to solicit a specific response; you are asking because God calls you to do it (Matthew 5:23-24).

Oh, friend, we are implored as chosen, holy and beloved children (Colossians 3:12) to put on kindness. God loves you and your spouse. He has saved you by the precious blood of His Son. If you and your spouse are believers in Christ then you both are part of the body of Christ; the same mercy of God chose you, the same grace of God saved you, the same blood of the Lamb bought you. It is only right that we extend the same kindness that we have received from our great and kind Heavenly Father, through His Son and His Spirit.

As I learned this lesson, I began to show kindness to my husband in a variety of ways, such as:

- Speaking kindly to him,
- Helping him to understand his forgiveness in Christ as well as to feel my forgiveness toward him,
- Showing him that I loved him and wanted to help him,
- Writing loving notes to him,
- Showing him that I desired him spiritually, emotionally, and sexually.

Some of my acts of kindness were ignored, some were well received, and some were rejected outright; but by God's grace, I am continuing to grow in this area regardless of the outcome.

> **Question 6:** How can you show gospel-centered kindness toward your spouse today? Please be specific:
>
> _____
>
> _____
>
> _____
>
> _____

Tomorrow, we will move on to consider our next Christian grace: humility. Until then, I pray that you will remember the kindness of Christ toward you—the One Who called you before time began, Who loves you and gave Himself for you, Who rose to justify you, Who promises to keep you to the end—and then extend that same type of kindness to your spouse today.

Cross-Focused Humility

Welcome back to the A United Front course where we are studying God's Word to become a united front with our spouse against the attacks of the world, the flesh, and the devil.

In recent lessons, we've been studying Colossians 3:12-13. So far, we've explored the attributes of a compassionate heart and kindness. God, the Father, demonstrated both when He sent Jesus who died to forgive our sins, restore our relationship with God, and give us eternal life with Him. We understood that as forgiven, holy, beloved children of God, we are to put on these attributes of Christ. And we put on compassionate hearts and kindness by looking to Christ and His cross, for as we "behold" Him we transform into His image.

Now, let's review Colossians 3:12-13 to uncover the next gospel characteristic to which we are called:

> *"Put on then, as God's chosen ones, holy and beloved, compassionate hearts, kindness, humility, meekness, and patience, bearing with one another and, if one has a complaint against another, forgiving each other; as the Lord has forgiven you, so you also must forgive."*
> *Colossians 3:12-13*

Question 1: According to Colossians 3, after a compassionate heart and kindness what are we to put on as God's chosen ones?
- ☐ A strong mind
- ☐ A thick skin
- ☐ Humility

According to vs. 12, we are to put on "humility", or other translations read "*lowliness of mind.*" I find it easiest to understand humility when considering Christ. To get a better understanding of what it means to be humble, let us consider Philippians 2:5-9, *"Have this mind among yourselves, which is yours in Christ Jesus, who, though he was in the form of God, did not count equality with God a thing to be grasped, but emptied himself, by taking the form of a servant, being born in the likeness of men. And being found in human form, he humbled himself by becoming obedient to the point of death, even death on a cross. Therefore, God has highly exalted him and bestowed on him the name that is above every name,"*

> **Question 2:** We are to have the same mind as Christ. According to Philippians 2:5-9, how did Christ humble Himself?
> ☐ By being poor and working with fisherman.
> ☐ By emptying Himself of glory, taking on the form of a servant and being obedient to the point of dying on the cross.
> ☐ By eating with tax collectors and sinners.

Oh, dear friend, take a moment and meditate on the humility of Christ in this passage. Jesus—Lord of heaven and earth—humbled Himself and became a helpless human baby born to a lowly Jewish family under Roman rule. The Word of God became flesh (John 1:1)!

As if this humble birth were not enough, Jesus purposefully became a servant. He "emptied Himself, taking the form of a servant." Jesus "came not to be served, but to serve, and give His life a ransom for many" (Matthew 20:28).

And then He humbled Himself lower still by becoming obedient to the point of death. Our Jesus said to the Father, *"Not my will, but Yours be done" (Luke 42:22b)* in the Garden of Gethsemane. Though the agony of soul was great, He yielded in obedience to the Father.

But the humbling was even more significant than death; Christ humbled Himself so low to die a criminal's death *on a cross.* Crucifixion was known to be the worst sort of death—torturous and agonizing—and reserved for the worst criminals.

Paul describes it in Galatians 3, *"Christ redeemed us from the curse of the law by becoming a curse for us—for it is written, "Cursed is everyone who is hanged on a tree." (Galatians 3:13).*

Jesus—pure, perfect, righteous, worthy, beloved, just, and holy Lamb of God—became a curse for you so that you might become the righteousness of God. Now, you are a child of God, free from the curse of separation from God because of Christ's humble sacrifice. You enjoy the presence and power of God because Christ took your sinfulness and gave you His righteousness. As I consider the humility of Christ, my heart aches with gratitude.

When I uncovered my husband's sin, my pride was evident in how I looked down on him for his failure. I was high-minded, thinking that I was better because I didn't sin in the same way. This prideful attitude remained until I was challenged by a true friend to examine my heart before the Lord. What I saw in my own heart (my sin struggles) humbled me and created a desire in me to walk the road of repentance *with* my husband instead of looking down at him judgmentally from the high road of pride.

Several years ago, a woman wrote to me very upset about what she called her husband's "convenient conversion." The husband, a professing believer, active and respected in their church, was secretly involved with immorality. When everything was uncovered, the man was devastated and told the pastor that he didn't believe he had ever been truly converted because he had always been living a double life. At this point, he confessed his sins, sought forgiveness, made a profession of faith and was baptized.

The whole church was rejoicing, but the wife was furious. She said she couldn't believe her husband was going to "get away with all he had done," all because of his "convenient conversion." I gently pointed out that every conversion is "convenient" for the sinner, but no conversions are cheap; they cost our Lord His life. Yes, her husband sinned, but so do we all. We all have sinned and deserve death and hell, but we don't receive what we deserve because of Christ's finished work on the cross.

I urged her to remember Christ and His words in Luke 15:10, *"Just so, I tell you, there is joy before the angels of God over one sinner who repents."* If there is joy in Heaven when a sinner repents then certainly there should be joy in the church, in our homes and in our hearts when anyone (especially our spouse) repents. To view repentance any other way reveals sin in our own hearts. Christ humbled Himself and died on the cross for all of our sins; *it is the height of pride to desire or demand a higher payment for sins than His precious blood.*

Question 3: After considering the humility of Christ, have you been humble in your attitude towards your spouse? Please share.

_____

_____

_____

_____

Jesus displayed this essential attribute of humility to His disciples in a very vivid way. We can read the full account in John 13, but in short, Jesus was fellowshipping with His disciples at the table then He got up, left his place at the head of the table, laid aside His outer garments and clothed Himself with a towel, taking on the form of a servant. Imagine the Lord of Heaven clothed in a servant's towel!

And this was just a little picture of what Christ has already done. In the beginning, Jesus was fellowshipping in Heaven with His Father, then He laid aside His glory and humbled Himself by coming down to us, wrapped in a human body.

Then Jesus astounded his disciples by washing their dirty feet with the towel wrapped around His waist. The disciples were shocked! It seemed too much to take in, that their Lord would humble Himself in this way. That the holy Lord, the pure and spotless Lamb of God, was willing to get dirty to make them clean. What humility! What love!

Dear friend, just as Jesus cleansed the disciples' feet, He would soon wash them (and us), becoming filthy with their (and our) sins on the cross, to make us all holy and righteous. The pure and innocent One would purposefully become defiled and dirty, to cleanse the ones He loves.

Finally, Jesus returned to His place at the table of fellowship, having cleansed the feet of His disciples. Again, the picture is clear: having made atonement for our sins Jesus would soon rise from the dead and return to the Father. _"After making purification for sins, He sat down at the right hand of the Majesty on high" (Hebrews 1:3b)._

This story is so impacting to me. The Lord of glory washing dirty feet! And these were truly dirty feet that the disciples had; this wasn't some symbolic act that Jesus was doing. At that time, men wore sandals or walked barefoot on dirty roads which would have been littered with animal waste and other unpleasantness. Foot washing was usually the job of the lowest servant in the household.

Today, we might not need our feet washed, but we certainly need to be washed and cleansed from our sin and the filth of this world.

> **Question 4:** How does Jesus humbling Himself to the point of washing you clean through His death on the cross affect your heart? Please share.

As we appreciate the humility of and rejoice in the love of Jesus, let us remember the closing words Jesus spoke to the disciples in John 13:13-15, *"Do you understand what I have done to you? You call me Teacher and Lord, and you are right, for so I am. If I then, your Lord and Teacher, have washed your feet, you also ought to wash one another's feet. For I have given you an example, that you also should do just as I have done to you."*

Jesus said that He had given His disciples an example. We, too, should follow Christ in humility by:

- Washing at the cross, communicating it in word and deed. There is no cleansing apart from Christ and His death; if we would see our spouse walking in purity, then we must bring them to the place of cleansing—the cross of Christ.
- Meeting the need of the one who is "dirty." The disciples had dirty feet, so Jesus humbled himself to that service, and we should adapt our ministry to the need at hand.

My husband did not need his physical feet washed, but he had other needs. I began to minister to him by spending time with him doing the things he enjoys, trying to say "Yes" to him whenever possible. Doing this was sometimes inconvenient for me but always helpful to our marriage. I sought to make our home a refuge from the world and to engage my husband's body, mind, and spirit.

It wasn't easy; but having the humble mind of Christ which says, *"I will serve you and help to bring about cleanliness, purity, love, and joy in your life. I will lower myself so that you might benefit"* is a fruitful and blessed way of life.

Question 5: How can you follow Jesus' example and minister to your spouse today? Please share.

_____

_____

_____

_____

May the humility of your Savior who did not cling to His equality with the Father but humbled Himself willingly to become your atoning sacrifice enable the same attitude in your heart.

Learning Meekness

Welcome back to the A United Front course. I pray your heart is being encouraged as you study and that you are experiencing healing in your heart and marriage.

In our previous lesson, we considered what it meant to put on cross-focused humility. We learned about "having the mind of Christ" by actively pursuing humility in our relationship with God and others, especially our spouse. We do this by lowering ourselves to serve those who are dirty and undeserving.

Christ humbled Himself by emptying Himself of His glory, taking on the form of a man, living as a servant and then dying on the cross as a criminal. Jesus lived the life we should have lived and then died the death that we deserved. He lowered Himself to the point of death on a criminal's cross so that we, dirty and undeserving, might be cleansed and made righteous.

Christ gave us an example of humility to follow by taking on the form of a servant and washing the filthy feet of His disciples. We follow Him when we humbly serve others and meet their needs, helping them to live in Light and love of Jesus.

Let's read Colossians 3:12-13 again and continue in our study:

> *"Put on then, as God's chosen ones, holy and beloved, compassionate hearts, kindness, humility, meekness, and patience, bearing with one another and, if one has a complaint against another, forgiving each other; as the Lord has forgiven you, so you also must forgive. And above all these put on love, which binds everything together in perfect harmony." Colossians 3:12-13*

So far, we have discussed putting on compassionate hearts, kindness, and humility. Today, we will discuss what it means to put on meekness.

Meekness is similar to humility, gentleness, and submission, but it is distinct from these. *Meekness is restrained power*; it is yielding and suffers injury without resentment or bitterness. It is best understood when looking at Christ.

Indeed, the beautiful thing about all the qualities mentioned in Colossians 3 is that we learn them all from Jesus. We only need to keep our eyes on Christ to be transformed little by little into His image. We don't have to try and figure out what Jesus would do; instead, we look to and consider what Christ has done on our behalf and this informs our response to others and our circumstances. As we behold and rest in Jesus, He will work in and through us. Jesus said, "*Take my yoke upon you, and learn from me, for I am gentle and lowly in heart, and you will find rest for your souls." (Matthew 11:29)*

So, let's do that now, let's sit at the feet of Jesus, learn about meekness from Him, and find rest for our souls. Please read with me Luke 9:51-56 NASB:

> *When the days were approaching for His ascension, He was determined to go to Jerusalem; and He sent messengers on ahead of Him, and they went and entered a village of the Samaritans to make arrangements for Him. But they did not receive Him, because He was traveling toward Jerusalem. When His disciples James and John saw this, they said, "Lord, do You want us to command fire to come down from heaven and consume them?" But He turned and rebuked them, and said, "You do not know what kind of spirit you are of; for the Son of Man did not come to destroy men's lives, but to save them." And they went on to another village.*

Question 1: In Luke 9, we see that Jesus was traveling with His disciples to Jerusalem where He would die on the cross as an atoning sacrifice for our sins. On the way, Jesus was rejected by a town of Samaritans. According to Luke 9:54, what did James and John ask Jesus?
- ☐ Do you want us to feed them?
- ☐ Do you want us to lead them in worship?
- ☐ Do you want us to call down fire from heaven and consume them?

James and John were greatly offended by these Samaritans who rejected Jesus. The disciples were so upset they asked Jesus if He wanted them to call down fire from heaven and consume the sinners! Destroying our offender might sound extreme, but we spouses might be tempted to respond aggressively, too, when faced with a spouse who has rejected us. Nevertheless, we can see in Luke 9:55 that Jesus rebukes the disciples for reacting in the flesh and forgetting Him and His mission.

> **Question 2:** According to Luke 9:56, what did Jesus come to do? Fill in the blank. *for the Son of Man did not come to destroy men's lives, but* _____ _____ _____."

Jesus did not come to destroy lives but to save them. Dear friend, do you see the meekness of Jesus here? Omnipotent Jesus restrained His power and explained to His disciples that there was another way to deal with sinners, another way to deal with sin. **He is the way!** Jesus does not destroy the sinner; He dies for the sinner. Here Jesus displays meekness gloriously. Jesus accepted the Samaritan's rejection without resentment or bitterness; He set aside His feelings for a higher purpose - our salvation.

As I consider the meekness of Christ, I am in awe and filled with gratitude for my meek and humble Savior. I was just like the Samaritans; rejecting the One that would save me. I deserved the fire of God's wrath, but my Jesus saved me. He took all the fiery wrath of God upon Himself because that was His mission. My heart is full of thankfulness; I hope that yours is as well.

> **Question 3:** How does considering the meekness of Christ affect your heart? Please share.

Now, let's look again at the meekness of Jesus as displayed in a different situation. Read John 8:2-11:

> *"Early in the morning he came again to the temple. All the people came to him, and he sat down and taught them. The scribes and the Pharisees brought a woman who had been caught in adultery, and placing her in the midst they said to him, "Teacher, this woman has been caught in the act of adultery. Now in the Law Moses commanded us to stone such women. So, what do you say?" This they said to test him, that they might have some charge to bring against him. Jesus bent down and wrote with his finger on the ground. And as they continued to ask him, he stood up and said to them, "Let him who is without sin among you be the first to throw a stone at her." And once more he bent down and wrote on the ground. But when they heard it, they went away one by one, beginning with the older ones, and Jesus was left alone with the woman standing before him. Jesus stood up and said to her, "Woman, where are they? Has no one condemned you?" She said, "No one, Lord." And Jesus said, "Neither do I condemn you; go, and from now on sin no more.""* John 8: 2-11

Question 4: Considering what we've learned so far in this lesson, what do you learn about meekness from the account of Jesus and the woman caught in adultery?

_____

_____

_____

_____

Let's acknowledge up front that this woman committed adultery; she had sinned grievously. Jesus does not dispute the sinfulness of the woman, but there is a vast difference between the Pharisees' response to the sinner woman and

Jesus' response to her. It is in Jesus' response that we see not only His love for the sinner, His grace and kindness to her, but also His meekness.

The Pharisees wanted to stone this woman because the Law said she deserved death for her sin of adultery. Jesus does not dispute this fact; nor should we, because the wages of sin is death (Romans 6:23). But Jesus dealt with the situation differently because He had a different mission from the Law.

The Law uncovers sin; Jesus saves from sin.

Jesus was the only One present at the "trial" who could have justly condemned the woman and put her to death (as He was the only One without sin), but He did not do it. He did not condemn her, but rather, He forgave her and then invited her to leave her sinful life.

Meekness is strength under control, power restrained. In the first passage, we looked at today Jesus had the power to destroy those who rejected Him, but He restrained that power because He did not come to destroy lives but to save them. In the second passage, Jesus had the authority to condemn and destroy the sinful woman, yet He refused to use that power and chose to forgive and not condemn.

Now, let's apply this matter of meekness to our own lives. Perhaps your spouse has rejected you in the past or has committed physical adultery like the woman in John 8. Some would encourage you to react in the flesh and seek to destroy your spouse or at least publicly shame and condemn them.

But Jesus has another way. His way is the way of grace, love, and forgiveness - the way of meekness. Having the power to destroy, humiliate, and condemn yet choosing to forgive and restore instead. Jesus does not condemn you for your sins; nor does He want you to condemn others for their sins.

Jesus calls us to a meek attitude of the heart that does not condemn the sinner but instead encourages and enables their repentance. Those who do not have the Spirit of Christ or the mind of Christ will tell us to kick the sinner to the curb or make them pay for what they've done. But Jesus, who died on the cross for your sins and those of your spouse too, says to forgive and live in meekness. God has given us all we need for life and godliness in His Word; we can reject the world's counsel because we have the better part in Him (Luke 10:42) and no one can separate us from His love (Romans 8:38-39).

Question 5: In considering the two biblical accounts of Jesus' meekness that you read in this lesson, do you have a heart of meekness toward your spouse? Please share.

_____

_____

_____

_____

Patience and Forbearance through Jesus

*H*ello and welcome back to the A United Front course. In this lesson, we will continue toward the goal of becoming a united front with our spouse against the attacks of the devil, the weakness of the flesh and the allurements of this world.

We've been considering Colossians 3:12-14 and so far, we've studied what it means to put on compassionate hearts, kindness, humility, and meekness. We have seen that all these attributes can be learned from Christ by looking to and considering His finished work on Calvary. What a precious Savior we have who not only saves us from sin but also works in us and wills us to live in this new way of Spirit-filled living.

Let's refer back to Colossians 3:12-14 and continue in our study:

> *"Put on then, as God's chosen ones, holy and beloved, compassionate hearts, kindness, humility, meekness, and patience, bearing with one another and, if one has a complaint against another, forgiving each other; as the Lord has forgiven you, so you also must forgive. And above all these put on love, which binds everything together in perfect harmony." Colossians 3:12-14*

Question 1: According to Colossians 3:12-13, we are to put on compassionate hearts, kindness, humility, meekness and _____, bearing with one another.

☐ Patience
☐ Pity
☐ Personality

Ah, patience! Solomon wrote, *"Better is the end of a thing than its beginning, and the patient in spirit is better than the proud in spirit." Ecclesiastes 7:8*

Standing on the other side of this trial and heartache which you are now navigating, I can say truly "the end of it" is indeed better than its beginning. I can also assure you that if you will trust in God and comfort yourself with the hope of the gospel through this challenging time, you will grow in the area of patience.

Patience (or more literally longsuffering) is undoubtedly a characteristic which must be cultivated and learned at the feet of Jesus. You may have also noticed in your reading of Colossians 3:12-13 that linked with patience is the phrase "bearing with one another," or some versions say, "forbearing."

These two qualities—patience and forbearance—are like two sides of the same coin. The first side, patience indicates an optimistic restraint—holding back your frustration or negative feelings with the hope that things will change. While the second side, forbearance or "bearing with one another" means to "hold oneself up" while waiting for change.

In short, the encouragement to you is: don't sink, hold on, be patient with your spouse.

None of us are born patient or forbearing. We must learn it. So, come with me now to Jesus, the One Whose burden is light and Whose yoke is easy, the One from Whom we may learn these traits which will serve our hearts and marriages well.

Look with me at Luke 13: 6-9:

> *And he told this parable: "A man had a fig tree planted in his vineyard, and he came seeking fruit on it and found none. And he said to the vinedresser, 'Look, for three years now I have come seeking fruit on this fig tree, and I find none. Cut it down. Why should it use up the ground?' And he answered him, 'Sir, let it*

alone this year also, until I dig around it and put on manure. Then if it should bear fruit next year, well and good; but if not, you can cut it down.'"

Question 2: In Luke 13:7, Jesus tells a parable; what did the owner of the vineyard want to do with the fig tree that did not bear fruit?
- ☐ Leave it alone.
- ☐ Climb it.
- ☐ Cut it down.

The owner said, "Look, this tree hasn't produced any fruit for over three years. Why should it take up space in my vineyard; **cut it down**."

Question 3: In Luke 13:8, what did the vinedresser ask to do with the barren tree?
- ☐ The vinedresser wanted to cut down the tree.
- ☐ The vinedresser wanted to give the tree more time and attention.
- ☐ The vinedresser wanted to move the tree to a new location.

The vinedresser entreated the owner on behalf of the tree. He said, "Give me one more chance with this tree. Let me do some work and amend the soil. And if my work isn't successful, then you can cut it down."

Now rather than debating all the potential meanings of this parable, I will ask you to focus today on the patience of God and the intercession of Jesus, as it is illustrated here for us in this parable.

We can see the patience of the owner of the vineyard from the beginning; after all, he waited three years for that tree to bear fruit. It isn't as if the owner was harsh or unreasonable. And yet, the vinedresser asked for more time. The vinedresser did not argue that the tree was worth saving or that the owner was wrong to expect fruit. No, the vinedresser knew that the tree deserved to be cut down; but he interceded based on the work that he, the vinedresser, planned to do.

Dear friend, we have a very patient Father in Heaven (the owner); but He is also just. God gave His perfect law, and every one of us failed to fulfill it. We were dead in our sins and fruitless. But God, in the person of Jesus (the Vinedresser), devised a way for us to be transformed from worthless people who deserved to be cut down into glorious and fruitful trophies of His grace.

Just think of this: Jesus came to you and did all the work: He did the suffering, became sin, took on all God's wrath, sowed His own body into the ground, all so that you could receive life and bear fruit. Because of Jesus and His work, God spared you and I. Hallelujah, what a Savior!

> **Question 4:** Have you experienced the patience of God in your life which led to your salvation and now your ongoing transformation? Please share.

It is essential for you to remember God's patience in your own life so that you will have the right perspective when it comes to being patient with your brothers and sisters in Christ, especially your spouse.

As we close out this lesson, let us consider some clarifying thoughts related to patience and forbearance within the context of dealing with habitual sin in our marriages.

Putting on patience does *not* mean that we ignore habitual sin in the marriage. In previous lessons, we have studied the Biblical response to habitual sin in marriage as given in Matthew 18. It is vital that we first implement the means of grace that God has given, and then we wait patiently and expectantly for the Lord to work.

Living in patience with our spouse does mean that we respond graciously if our spouse stumbles and falls just as we would have them do for us when we sin against them. We should not expect instant perfection.

Bearing with our spouse does *not* mean that:

- we just put up with them
- we live as martyrs making sure everyone knows how much we suffer in our marriages.

Bearing with our spouse *does* mean that:

- we respond with encouragement when we see our spouse struggling to overcome.
- we do whatever we can to help our spouse even if it is not convenient or it requires sacrifice on our part.

I learned this lesson the hard way. I was so impatient with my husband when he was first coming into purity. I wanted him to hurry up and get over his sin struggle so I pushed him to do the things I thought would be helpful (attending men's group, going to seminars, etc.), but things just seemed to get worse.

The harder I tried to "encourage" my husband to do what I thought he should be doing, the more he seemed to struggle and fall in his efforts to overcome.

I was so frustrated, and I often complained to God asking Him to do something because all the ways I tried to help my husband seemed to fail.

And then one day as I was reading my Bible and praying, God spoke to me through the book of Habakkuk. It is a short book in the Old Testament, and I recommend that you read it today if you have the time. Basically, Habakkuk complained to God, much as I was, "How long, O Lord?" and God told Habakkuk to hold on and wait…change would be coming. God told Habakkuk, *"Look among the nations, and see; wonder and be astounded. For I am doing a work in your days that you would not believe if told." Habakkuk 1:5*

And the message came through to me that I just needed to be patient and wait. I needed to trust that God was working in my husband's heart as well as in my heart. And now looking back, I know that if anyone had told me what a marvelous work that God was going to do in my marriage, I would not have believed it.

Dear friend, this is true for you, too. God is working. Be patient. Trust in Him; rest in Him.

You should encourage your spouse but not pressure them or demand results. You must wait on the Lord and believe that God will work in your situation and bring a resolution that is for your good and His glory.

> **Question 5:** Do you struggle with being patient or bearing with others? Explain.

_____

_____

_____

_____

Peter wrote of God's patient heart: *"The Lord is not slow to fulfill his promise as some count slowness, but is patient toward you, not wishing that any should perish, but that all should reach repentance." (2 Peter 3: 9 ESV)* Notice that God is patient with sinners. He patiently waits for us to repent and grants us repentance in His time (2 Timothy 2:25).

This patience toward the sinner is to be our heart for one another as well: we want to remain optimistically patient and wait on God to do His work in the heart of our spouse.

Let your heart be warmed and encouraged by God's long-suffering attitude toward you today, for as you do this, His patience will fill you up and flow from His heart to those around you.

> **Question 6:** How can you demonstrate patience and forbearance with your spouse today?

_____

_____

_____

_____

Forgiveness Learned
at the Cross

*W*elcome back to the A United Front course, friend.

You are three weeks into the study now! I pray that you are doing well and experiencing the grace of God in your heart as you study through the lessons. Now, let us return to Colossians 3:12-14 and continue in our study:

> *Put on then, as God's chosen ones, holy and beloved, compassionate hearts, kindness, humility, meekness, and patience, bearing with one another and, if one has a complaint against another, forgiving each other; as the Lord has forgiven you, so you also must forgive. And above all these put on love, which binds everything together in perfect harmony. Colossians 3:12-14*

Question 1: According to Colossians 3:13, how are you to forgive others?
- ☐ As they have forgiven you.
- ☐ As the Lord has forgiven you.
- ☐ As the church has forgiven you.

We are to forgive others as the Lord has graciously forgiven us. In earlier lessons, we have reminded ourselves of the forgiveness we have before God because of the atoning death of Jesus on the cross. And in light of this great forgiveness we have received from God, we must forgive those who sin against us. Extending forgiveness is not optional for us as Christians, and it is not dependent upon our feelings. We forgive others because we have been forgiven God.

Today, we will delve deeper into this subject of forgiveness by considering God's protection which frees us to forgive, and then we will end by looking at a vivid biblical illustration of forgiveness to learn very practical ways we can show forgiveness to our spouse.

First, let's consider *Romans 12:19 (NIV): "Do not take revenge, my friends, but leave room for God's wrath, for it is written: "It is mine to avenge; I will repay," says the Lord."*

> **Question 2:** In Colossians 3:13, we are instructed to forgive those who sin against us. In Romans 12:19 NIV, what are we told not to do when others sin against us?
> ☐ Do not let it happen again.
> ☐ Do not let anyone know what happened.
> ☐ Do not take revenge.

We are told not to take revenge on others when they sin against us because God is our Avenger! Dear friend, God sees your situation, and He cares. He knows every wrong ever done to you, and He can address those who offend you in ways that you cannot.

When someone sins against you, it is common to feel anger and to experience a desire to retaliate. But remember, these vengeful feelings originate in your flesh; they are not what you learned from Jesus. You must resist the urge to get even. Instead, you want to trust God to deal with any offense, and with all who offend.

Many people believe that they cannot or should not forgive their spouse too quickly or repeatedly because then the spouse might think their sin was a small thing, or that it didn't really matter, or that it is alright to do it again. But God assures us that this is not the case.

We can forgive generously because we know that God is going to deal with the one who has sinned against us. This should not impede our taking the steps of Matthew 18 when needed (as discussed in earlier lessons), but it does allow us to freely forgive knowing that God will discipline the one who has sinned.

Question 3: Considering your situation, are you living in forgiveness with your spouse and trusting in God as the Avenger of all wrongs? Please share:

_____

_____

_____

_____

So, we've established that as Christians, we do not take revenge, but now let's consider what we are to do. Romans 12:20-21, _"To the contrary, "...if your enemy is hungry, feed him; if he is thirsty, give him something to drink; for by so doing you will heap burning coals on his head." Do not be overcome by evil but overcome evil with good."_

We can see a beautiful illustration of overcoming evil with good in the life of Joseph (Genesis 37-50). For the purpose of this lesson, I will provide a brief summary of the life of Joseph, and then we will consider how we might apply the biblical principles we see displayed in his life to our own:

Joseph was one of the twelve sons of Jacob. Joseph was greatly loved by his father but hated by his brothers. As a young man, he was sent out by his father to check on his brothers, but when they saw him coming, they plotted against him. They plotted his death originally, but instead sold him into the hands of Ishmaelites for pieces of silver. Joseph was then taken to Egypt and sold as a slave to work in the house of Potiphar (Genesis 37-38).

While in Potiphar's house, Joseph was falsely accused of a crime he did not commit and subsequently thrown into prison where he remained for many years (Genesis 39-40). Then, through a set of divinely inspired circumstances, Joseph was brought up from the prison and exalted to the right hand of Pharaoh.

A few years after Joseph came to power, a severe famine came upon the land which resulted in Joseph's brothers coming to Egypt for food. His brothers did not recognize Joseph when they knelt before him and requested to buy food for their families, but Joseph did recognize his brothers (Genesis 42-44).

In Genesis 45, we read of how Joseph revealed his identity and responded to his brothers who had sinned against him so grievously:

"Then Joseph said to his brothers, "Come close to me." When they had done so, he said, "I am your brother Joseph, the one you sold into Egypt! And now, do not be distressed and do not be angry with yourselves for selling me here, because it was to save lives that God sent me ahead of you. For two years now there has been famine in the land, and for the next five years there will not be plowing and reaping. But God sent me ahead of you to preserve for you a remnant on earth and to save your lives by a great deliverance. "So then, it was not you who sent me here, but God. He made me father to Pharaoh, lord of his entire household and ruler of all Egypt. Now hurry back to my father and say to him, 'This is what your son Joseph says: God has made me lord of all Egypt. Come down to me; don't delay. You shall live in the region of Goshen and be near me—you, your children and grandchildren, your flocks and herds, and all you have. I will provide for you there, because five years of famine are still to come. Otherwise you and your household and all who belong to you will become destitute.'… And he kissed all his brothers and wept over them. Afterward his brothers talked with him… So, the sons of Israel did this. Joseph gave them carts, as Pharaoh had commanded, and he also gave them provisions for their journey. To each of them he gave new clothing, but to Benjamin he gave three hundred shekels of silver and five sets of clothes. And this is what he sent to his father: ten donkeys loaded with the best things of Egypt, and ten female donkeys loaded with grain and bread and other provisions for his journey." Genesis 45:4-11,15, 21-23 (NIV)

Question 4: Please fill in the blanks. "if your _____ is hungry, _____ him; if he is thirsty, give him something to _____; for by so doing you will heap burning coals on his head." Do _____ _____ _____by evil but overcome evil with _____." Romans 12:20-21

Question 5: As you think about this story, how did Joseph evidence obedience to Romans 12:20-21 in responding to his brothers?

_____

_____

_____

_____

Joseph showed his forgiveness to his brothers by repaying their evil deeds with specific demonstrations of kindness. Joseph's brothers had planned to let him starve and die in a pit, but Joseph gave them food and a place to live well. His brothers tore off his beautiful coat, but Joseph gave them new clothes (v. 22). His brothers sold Joseph into slavery and sent him away, but Joseph said to them, "Come close to me" (v. 4) and saved them and their families from starvation. The brothers mocked and despised Joseph, he loved them and comforted them (v.6).

Joseph was in a position to take revenge on his brothers, but he didn't because, during his years of struggle, God had taught Joseph a different way of thinking and responding to his circumstances. Rather than strike back at his brothers, Joseph extended forgiveness, mercy, and grace.

Joseph even reassured his brothers, saying, "God sent me ahead of you." Essentially, he told them, "What you did was wrong, but I'm not angry with you because I know that it was all part of God's plan for my life." Sin is always sin and never excusable, but God works out all things and uses them for His glory, even the sins of others against us.

Joseph didn't just forgive his brothers verbally either. He evidenced his whole-hearted forgiveness when he returned blessings for curses and overcame evil with good.

We too are called to "forgive as we've been forgiven" and "overcome evil with good."

With Christ living in you, you will:

- pray for the forgiveness of those who hurt you
- bless those who curse you
- do good to those who do evil to you
- love those who hate you

And as you do, you will evidence that you are forgiving as you have been forgiven.

> **Question 6:** How can you show forgiveness and overcome evil with good in your marriage? Please share.

_____

_____

_____

_____

In closing, let's remember Jesus who as He was dying on the cross, prayed for those who mistreated Him and did good to those who crucified Him.

Like Joseph, Jesus was rejected by His brothers, sold into the hands of Gentiles for pieces of silver. Like Joseph, Jesus was falsely accused and placed between two criminals. And, like Joseph, Jesus was lifted up and exalted to the place of Lord, being the Savior of all who come to Him.

There is no more excellent example of overcoming evil with good than our precious Savior who became sin (evil) for us so that we might become the righteousness (good) of God (2 Corinthians 5:21). If we need additional encouragement towards forgiveness, we only need to look at Jesus and remember the enormous debt of sin of which we have been forgiven so that we might go and do likewise.

Living in the Love of Jesus

*G*ood day, friend, and welcome back to the A United Front course.

This lesson will conclude our study in Colossians 3:12-14, but I encourage you to continue meditating on the passage as there is so much more to learn from it.

> *Put on then, as God's chosen ones, holy and beloved, compassionate hearts, kindness, humility, meekness, and patience, bearing with one another and, if one has a complaint against another, forgiving each other; as the Lord has forgiven you, so you also must forgive. And above all these put on love, which binds everything together in perfect harmony. Colossians 3:12-14*

Question 1: So far, we have studied what it means to put on compassionate hearts, kindness, humility, meekness, patience, forbearance and forgiveness. According to Colossians 3:14, what do we put on above all of these?
- ☐ Happiness
- ☐ Laughter
- ☐ Love

Question 2: According to Colossians 3:14, what does love do? Please fill in the blank. *And above all these put on love, which _____ _____ _____in perfect harmony.*

We are to put on love, which binds everything—compassion, kindness, humility, meekness, patience, forbearance and forgiveness—together in perfect harmony. You might think of love as the belt that holds on all your gospel given clothes. Without biblical love, it all falls apart.

To be sure, this isn't the romance novel, romantic movie, love ballad foolishness that the world suggests is love. The world says, "I fell in love" or "I fell out of love." The world speaks ridiculous lies such as, "Love means never having to say you are sorry." The world regularly confuses infatuation and lust with love.

> **Question 3:** Can you think of some wrong ideas about love that you have been told or perhaps even believed at one time? Write them here.
>
> _____
>
> _____
>
> _____
>
> _____

With so many wrong ideas about love circulating in the world today, we as Christians are frequently tempted to believe lies about love which is harmful to our hearts and relationships. If we want to avoid this pitfall, we must look to God's Word for the clear and correct understanding of biblical love. If we want to combat the lies of the world, our flesh and the devil, then we must learn from Jesus what true love is.

1 John 3:16 (NIV) provides a clear definition for us: _"This is how we know what love is: Jesus Christ laid down his life for us. And we ought to lay down our lives for our brothers and sisters."_

> **Question 4:** According to 1 John 3:16, how can we know what love is? Fill in the blank. "_____ Christ _____ _____ his _____ for us."

Oh, friend, we know what love is when we see and understand what Christ did for us on the cross of Calvary. Christ's sacrificial death to save us is the benchmark of true love.

When my husband was first coming into purity, heartache filled our marriage, and in my pain, I believed the lies of the devil and not only doubted the love of my husband but also began to question the love of God. The devil tempted me with many thoughts such as, "If God loves you so then why did He let your husband go off into sin? Why are all these bad things happening to you? God doesn't love you. No one loves you. You must have done something terrible to deserve all this pain." These thoughts troubled and disturbed me for a long time until God gave me faith to believe Romans 8:38-39,

"For I am convinced that neither death nor life, neither angels nor demons, neither the present nor the future, nor any powers, neither height nor depth, nor anything else in all creation, will be able to separate us from the love of God that is in Christ Jesus our Lord." Romans 8:38-39 (NIV)

Clearly, our circumstances in this life are not the measure of God's love for us. It is at the cross of Christ, where we can see the height and depth of God's love for us, that is the true measure of God's love.

Look with me now at the cross and see Love (1 John 4:8) dying in your place. See the crown of thorns which pierced His head, the open gashes from the beating He received, the angry welts on his face where His beard was plucked out, and His face struck, see His hands and feet pierced through and the gaping wound in His side from which flowed His life's blood to provide payment for your sins. All this our precious Savior endured for your sake. Every mark is evidence and confirmation of His eternal love. Christ died so that you might know undying, life-transforming, soul-saving love!

Dear friend, do you know that you are deeply loved? Do you know that you are loved beyond words, loved beyond measure? You are loved perfectly and profoundly by God the Father; so much so that He sent His one and only Son Jesus to die on the cross to atone for your sins (John 3:16). You are loved deeply, richly, and eternally by the Lord of Glory, the precious Lamb of God who gave His own life to take away your sins (John 1:29). And what is more: nothing will ever, or could ever, separate you from His love (Romans 8: 31-39)! You are loved! Nothing anyone ever says, does, or does not do will ever change God's love for you. No one can take Him away from you (Song of Solomon 2:16).

It is immensely encouraging to bask in the love of God. I find that as I meditate on God's love for me and specifically on Christ's perfect display of love on the cross that my heart fills to overflowing and my mind can envision things it could not before.

God's love empowers! Where the flesh says, "I cannot!" God's love says, "It is finished!"

Before we close out this lesson, let's consider one final passage which will help us understand biblical love:

> *1 Corinthians 13:4-8, "Love is patient and kind; love does not envy or boast; it is not arrogant or rude. It does not insist on its own way; it is not irritable or resentful; it does not rejoice at wrongdoing but rejoices with the truth. Love bears all things, believes all things, hopes all things, endures all things. Love never ends."*

> **Question 5:** Please list out, in your own words, all the things love is and isn't according to 1 Corinthians 13:4-8:

As I read this passage in 1 Corinthians 13, I am struck by how much Jesus is all these things. Jesus is patient and kind. Jesus did not insist on His own way but submitted even to death on the cross. Jesus is the Truth Who died for our wrongdoings. Jesus endured all things for our sakes so that we could know love without end.

If we were to read all of 1 Corinthians 13, we would see the futility of doing good things apart from love, and this is what God is telling us in Colossians 3 as well. Apart from love, we cannot live with compassionate hearts, kindness, humility, meekness, patience, forbearance, and forgiveness. Without love, all our efforts to help our spouse will be a waste of time, energy, and effort.

Biblical love is costly. It involves dying. It is others focused. It is patient, kind, generous, enduring, full of hope, and never-ending. It is Jesus. It is impossible to have biblical love apart from Christ.

A wife once told me, "I would love him if I could, but I just can't. He has hurt me too much. I've tried all that stuff the Bible says, and it didn't work. I'm tired. I've endured enough. I'm going to tell my husband that when he changes, I'll try to make an effort again."

We can sympathize with this wife's struggle. Sin is fatiguing to our hearts and minds, which is why we must fortify our hearts and minds in the gospel of Jesus. We cannot love others biblically if we are not first receiving true love from Jesus as displayed through His death on His cross.

If you want to love biblically, you must believe in and receive Jesus' cross love for you and learn from Him how to lay down your life and love others.

This wife did not understand biblical love. She did not understand God's love for her. God didn't wait for her to get her act together before sending His Son to die in her place. Jesus didn't say, "Father, forgive them when they know and understand how terrible they are." This poor lady allowed her feelings of weariness and pain to control her mind instead of having the mind of Christ. It was no wonder she felt helpless to show love to her husband since she was not experiencing it from Christ. If biblical love binds everything together, then a lack of it drives people away from one another.

> **Worldly love pushes the sinner away until they change, but God's love (gospel love) draws the sinner near and binds hearts together.**

Gospel love empathizes with the struggle and believes that change is possible. Indeed, gospel love uses every means of grace available to encourage the sinning one toward repentance and restoration including applying all the biblical principles of Matthew 18 and even calling the local authorities if necessary. *Gospel love is generous, but it is not foolish.*

Question 6: How can you show biblical love to your spouse today?

_____

_____

_____

_____

Some ways I learned to show love to my husband are: listening to him, speaking words of encouragement and hope to him, focusing on his positive traits and commending him for them, speaking kindly about him to others, helping him with his work, going on hikes with him, following his lead, supporting his ideas, and showing physical affection to him—hugging, kissing, physical intimacy.

> *1 John 4:10-12, "In this is love, not that we have loved God but that he loved us and sent his Son to be the propitiation for our sins. Beloved, if God so loved us, we also ought to love one another. No one has ever seen God; if we love one another, God abides in us and his love is perfected in us."*

Question 7: How are things going in your marriage? Please share.

_____

_____

_____

_____

Friend, biblical love is the "most excellent way" of life (1 Corinthians 12:31); it fulfills the whole law of God (Romans 13:10). I pray that you will look to Jesus to know true love and that God will make love abound more and more (Philippians 1:9) in your heart and marriage.

Trust in Jesus

Welcome back to the A United Front course!

Recently, I received this inquiry from a wife: "How can I ever trust my husband again? I'm so afraid all the time that he is viewing pornography or chatting with women when he is online. Sometimes I will be in the other room, and the thoughts will come to my mind that he is sinning, so I run into the room and check his pulse. I know that when he is hiding something from me, his pulse goes up. But it doesn't help me to feel that his pulse is normal; I think he's only learned to hide his sin better. Also, sometimes my husband laughs at me when I do this, and he tells me I'm silly, and other times, he gets angry and tells me to stop it. I'm so confused. What should I do?"

My heart went out to this dear lady. When sin invades a marriage, it sows the seeds of mistrust and self-protection. These feelings are unwelcome, and our hearts cry out to be relieved of the burden. We all want to feel loved and safe in our marriages, but the injury of sin makes us wonder if we can ever trust our spouse again. Should we?

Well, in this lesson and the next, we will search the Scriptures for the best way to approach this issue of trust in our marriages.

Let's begin with a look at Jesus' approach to trust.

"Now when he was in Jerusalem at the Passover Feast, many believed in his name when they saw the signs that he was doing. But Jesus on his part did not entrust himself to them, because he knew all people and needed no one to bear witness about man, for he himself knew what was in man." John 2: 23-25

Question 1: According to John 2:24-25, why did Jesus not entrust himself to those who believed in Him?

☐ He knew all people

☐ He didn't need people

☐ He was afraid of getting hurt

Jesus knew what was in a person's heart, and he knew he could not trust them.

Notice here that the verse is not specific to the individuals present but rather the passage says, "*...he knew all people.*" Jesus knew that He could not entrust himself to people because of what was in them.

This fact prompts us to ask, "What was it in people that Jesus found untrustworthy?"

> "And he [Jesus] said, "What comes out of a person is what defiles him. For from within, out of the heart of man, come evil thoughts, sexual immorality, theft, murder, adultery, coveting, wickedness, deceit, sensuality, envy, slander, pride, foolishness. All these evil things come from within, and they defile a person." Mark 7:20-23*

We are each born in sin (Psalm 51:5; Ephesians 2:3) with hearts that are deceitful and wicked (Jeremiah 17:9). When we come to faith in Christ, we receive a new nature (2 Corinthians 5:17), but we still live in bodies of flesh which are weak (Mark 14:38). It should not surprise us then when *we* sin or *our spouse* sins. Betrayal began in the Garden of Eden with Adam and Eve, and it continues to this day. We cannot explicitly trust in anyone, but this does not mean that we go through life always waiting for "Judas' kiss." There is a better option.

Paul wrote in 1 Corinthians 13:7 that love *"hopes all things."* As gospel-centered spouses, we approach our marriage (all relationships) hoping the best; but not forgetting what is in a person—a heart of flesh that is weak and prone to sin.

When considering how another has broken your "trust," it is essential to remember that you are a promise-breaker too.

For years, my husband could never be sure if what would come out of my mouth would be edifying or not. I can remember times in conversations with others where I would be relating a story which would present myself as the wise one while my husband would appear hapless and inept. It didn't matter that what I said was true; the point was that I had betrayed my husband's trust by tearing him down in front of others. My foolish talk caused my husband to retreat from fellowship with others and me.

Question 2: Can you think of a time when you broke your spouse's trust? Please share.

_____

_____

_____

_____

At this point, you might be tempted to think that your failures toward your spouse are small in comparison with their grievous sin, but this type of thinking is not humble. Indeed, comparing ourselves to one another is unwise and a trap of the devil (2 Corinthians 10:12).

There are many ways in which we can break trust with our spouse. Sexual impurity is just one of many sins that can tear down a marriage. Belittling speech, overspending, gluttony, rage, drunkenness, sinful anger, etc. all these can tear down and even destroy a marriage (Proverbs 14:1).

So, we cannot unwaveringly trust ourselves or our spouse, but we can follow Christ and put our trust where He did.

"For to this you have been called, because Christ also suffered for you, leaving you an example, so that you might follow in his steps. He committed no sin, neither was deceit found in his mouth. When he was reviled, he did not revile in return; when he suffered, he did not threaten, but continued entrusting himself to him who judges justly." 1 Peter 2:21-23

Question 3: According to 1 Peter 2:23, to Whom did Jesus entrust himself when He was betrayed?

☐ His disciples
☐ Pontius Pilot
☐ God who judges justly

Ultimately, we can only safely put our trust in God. He alone can support such a high calling. Our spouses are never going to be able to overcome the fears, frustrations, and anxieties of our hearts. But God can, and He wants us to cast our anxieties on Him (1 Peter 5:7) because He cares for us!

We can safely trust in God *because He has proven His love for us*:

- Jesus died on the cross, took all the wrath of God that was due to us, rose again on the third day and is today interceding and preparing a place for us!
- The Holy Spirit lives in us, comforting and guiding us.
- Our God is Faithful and True; He can be trusted with everything.

Question 4: Do you trust God when it comes to your life and your marriage?

_____

_____

_____

_____

You can and should put your trust fully in God who judges justly. But you also want to work together with your spouse toward building a healthy, loving relationship where each person shows themselves to be as trustworthy as possible. The effort should never be a one-sided where your spouse tries to earn your trust by doing certain things or following rules you establish. It should always be a team effort.

A Christian marriage is to be centered on the gospel, not the law. The law says, "Measure up or die"; the gospel says, "You are forgiven; let's try again."

Galatians 3 tells us that all who rely on works of the law are under a curse and that no one can be justified before God by the law. God's people live by faith, not law.

Christ redeemed you from the curse of the law by becoming a curse for you when He hung on the cross and died in your place (Galatians 3:10-14). Christ fulfilled the law and removed it from you, making you free to live according to the gospel.

The relationship of the gospel-centered couple is not based on the merits or trustworthiness of each individual, but on Christ and His righteousness, which has been given to them both equally. This is why all the admonitions in the Bible for husbands (to love and provide) and wives (to be subject to and respect) are always surrounded by the message of the cross and resurrection of Jesus.

As a couple trusts in Christ to keep them, they can live in peace and grace with one another, knowing they are loved and accepted in Jesus and also with each other.

The Christian couple is safe in Christ, and because of Him, they are safe with one another.

Gospel acceptance and mutual dependence upon Christ create an environment that invites growth in grace and love for each other.

Question 5: Has your marriage been based on the righteousness of Christ or on your acts toward one another? Please share.

_____

_____

_____

_____

One of the best things a couple can do to begin rebuilding their marriage is to sit down with one another and discuss this topic openly. You might approach your spouse in this way:

> *"Honey, I'd like to work together with you on building up our marriage. Would you be willing to talk with me about how we can do this? Would you tell me what I can do to make you feel loved, respected, and valued?"*

Hopefully, this approach will be well received, and your spouse will reciprocate. If not, then go ahead with your part and revisit the topic later.

Your goal is to create a mutually safe and comfortable environment where both people feel valued. You want to work as a team. Some easy ideas are sharing computer history, sharing receipts, location sharing, sending frequent texts to each other.

Work together to identify areas where extra transparency will help bring comfort and reassurance to your hearts. If you have trouble with this exercise (you and your spouse disagree on what would be helpful or realistic), then you should seek the help of a pastor, mentor, or friend to assist you.

> **Question 6:** What are some things you and your spouse could do to mutually build trust in your marriage? Please share.

If your spouse is making an effort to restore your relationship (even the smallest effort), it is essential to encourage them for taking action on your behalf. Let them know that you appreciate what they are doing.

If you find that you are still struggling with anxieties and fears related to your spouse, then tomorrow's lesson should be a help. We will be discussing, in a practical way, what to do with those troublesome thoughts the evil one sends your way.

I pray that you have your hope and trust in God and that you are already working together with your spouse to rebuild your marriage. God is faithful; He can make you a strong and united front for His glory.

LESSON 24:

Taking Thoughts Captive

*W*elcome back to the A United Front course!

In lesson 23, we began a study dealing with the matter of trust and the proper way to approach this issue in a gospel-centered marriage. Today, we will continue our study with a focus on how to deal with troublesome thoughts that get lodged in our minds.

After I discovered my husband's impurity, I was distressed by all manner of fearful, angry, confused, and sad thoughts. I wondered about where my husband was and what he was doing when he wasn't with me. I feared that he was going to leave our family and me. I felt betrayed and unloved.

Question 1: Please share any recurrent troubling thoughts that you have had/are having.

_____

_____

_____

_____

Dear friend, our mind is a battleground. The evil one does all he can to attack us in our minds because how we think affects how we act (Proverbs 23:7). If we can be distracted from Christ and encouraged to focus on our pain and our fears, then the devil can make progress toward the destruction of our marriage. But there is a way to fight back!

2 Corinthians 10:3-5 (NIV) guides us:

"For though we live in the world, we do not wage war as the world does. The weapons we fight with are not the weapons of the world. On the contrary, they have divine power to demolish strongholds. We demolish arguments and every pretension that sets itself up against the knowledge of God, and we take captive every thought to make it obedient to Christ."

All believers are at war, but we do not fight as the world does. We fight with divine powered weapons!

Question 2: According to 2 Corinthians 10:4 NIV, what do these divine weapons demolish?
- ☐ Buildings
- ☐ Strongholds
- ☐ People

We Christians possess divine weapons to demolish demonic strongholds. A "*stronghold*" is an argument that "*sets itself up against the knowledge of God.*"

For example, worldly insights can become thought-strongholds in our minds. The world offers us "arguments" about "addiction" telling us our spouse will never change, but to believe the world's wisdom, we must deny the power of God.

Paul wrote to the Colossians that all true wisdom is in Christ, and warned them to reject the fine-sounding ideologies of the world:

My goal is that they may be encouraged in heart and united in love, so that they may have the full riches of complete understanding, in order that they may know the mystery of God, namely, Christ, in whom are hidden all the treasures of wisdom and knowledge. I tell you this so that no one may deceive you by fine-sounding arguments. Colossians 2:2-4 (NIV)

Thought strongholds are fine-sounding and always seem plausible at the moment, but again, to believe them, we must turn away from Christ and the power of the cross.

One thought stronghold I had was: "I am not what my husband needs. He needs someone sexier, smarter, and better than me. We should be with people who make us happy." This type of thinking was nearly my undoing. I feared I could never meet my husband's needs or make him happy. But now I know the truth; God has joined my husband and I together for a purpose. God can work in us to love and care for each other. God has united us to build His Kingdom. These are the truths that have replaced the lies I was believing.

> **Question 3:** Are there any beliefs about your life or marriage lodged in your mind that deny the power of God? Please share.

_____

_____

_____

_____

Thought strongholds can be dominating, debilitating, and frustrating. Another typical thought stronghold is the idea that when someone hurts us, we should hurt them back, so they learn not to hurt us. And in the world's economy this type of thinking makes sense, but not in God's.

While we were still sinners, Christ died for us. Jesus forgave all who betrayed Him while He was hanging on the cross suffering in their place. God calls us to bless those that curse us and to extend kindness and love to those who despitefully use us (Romans 12:14; Luke 6:28), and this is precisely what Jesus was doing on the cross!

If you would be free and have the mind of Christ, you must reject the ways of the world, your flesh, and the devil and instead cling to the cross, and walk by the truth of God's Word, in the power of God's Spirit.

> **Question 4:** Fill in the blank. *We demolish arguments and every pretension that sets itself up against the knowledge of God, and we _____ _____ every _____ to make it _____ to _____ (2 Corinthians 10:5 NIV).*

All believers have divine power to demolish demonic strongholds. This power flows from the Spirit of Christ, who lives in the believer.

Friend, you can knock down thought-strongholds by taking every thought captive and making it "obedient to Christ." The way you defeat your enemy is not by not thinking about your problems, but by thinking about Jesus! You examine your thoughts, and if they do not line up with the truth of the gospel, if they do not speak of forgiveness and the breaking of sin's power, you take it to Jesus and leave it with Him.

Practically speaking, as we are seeking restoration and healing in our marriages, we might have thoughts that begin to take shape in our minds. Evil thoughts. Discouraging thoughts. Even satanic thoughts. We learn to take those thoughts, each one of them, captive to Christ. We do not allow our thoughts to take us captive, rather we take them captive.

For example, if I were to have sudden thoughts of harming my spouse or myself, I would run to the cross with them and see Jesus' blood shed for me, and I would leave them at the throne of grace. I would remind myself that God's Word teaches me to bless those who curse me (Luke 6:28; Romans 12:14).

If I were to have thoughts of overeating, overspending or turning to alcohol for comfort, I would take those thoughts captive to Christ, seeing the cross as that which not only forgives my sin but also *crucifies my wrong desires* (Galatians 6:14). I would remind myself that Jesus calls me to receive my comfort from Him and His people (1 Peter 5:7; 2 Corinthians 1: 3-4).

Question 5: Why is it important to take our thoughts captive to Christ and see the power of the cross crucify those thoughts?

_____

_____

_____

_____

If we would be skillful at combating thought strongholds, we must continually remind ourselves of the truth of what Christ has done on our behalf through His death and resurrection and seeking to grow in our understanding of how to apply the gospel to our lives. Daily time in the Bible and prayer is as necessary for our spiritual life as breathing is to our physical one.

Question 6: Are you spending time in Bible study and prayer daily?
- ☐ Yes
- ☐ No
- ☐ Sometimes

Our passage today in 2 Corinthians 10 reminds us that there is a battle for our minds. Satan is active in presenting fine-sounding arguments much as he did with Eve in the Garden of Eden (Genesis 3:1-7). But we must never forget that his intentions are evil. His goal is to take us captive, keep us in bondage, and destroy our faith and our family. He wants us to respond to the sins committed against us in a sinful way. But we believers have the power of Christ Himself to demolish these arguments, obliterate them and destroy them by the power of God's Word and God's Spirit.

We must learn to reject all ideologies that are not rooted in the gospel of Jesus Christ; those that do not evidence faith. We examine every thought as to its source, and if not from God, we take it captive to Jesus Christ and leave it with Him. This is how we "take every thought captive to Christ" and thereby demolish demonic thought-strongholds. Specifically, we learn how to focus on the death and resurrection of Jesus, to fix our eyes on Jesus, to look at the cross and find our life in Him.

Today we saw from Scripture the extreme importance of demolishing all the "knowledge" and "fine-sounding arguments" that Satan wants to set up in our minds. The way to freedom is through taking every thought captive to Christ: we are to wash those thoughts away at the cross! Jesus took these thoughts and all your sins on Himself when He died on the cross and was buried in a tomb. Learn to rejoice in Jesus' resurrection power to free us from them! The cross demolishes these thoughts and washes them away!

As you first begin taking your thoughts captive to Christ, it may be hard to do, but it will become easier and more natural with practice (Hebrews 5:14). It won't be long before no evil idea can get set up in your mind as a stronghold because you will have formed a habit of taking all your thoughts to Christ to check them first.

In closing, I want to remind you that you are not alone. All Christians struggle with their thoughts sometimes. I can remember a time when I just wanted to die rather than face another day of wrestling with all the anguish and heartache in my life. I had trouble sleeping, eating, and relating to others because my mind was so clouded with the pain of my circumstances.

But God…in His great mercy showed me the way out of the darkness. He called me to listen to His voice and not the voices of my enemies - the world, my flesh, and the devil.

My enemies said untrue things: you are unworthy, no one loves you, no one wants you, you are ugly, you are stupid, you deserve better, you should run away.

But Jesus, the voice of Truth, spoke these good things to my heart:

- I love you!
- I sent my Son to die for your sins and those of the whole world. My grace is sufficient for you.
- I see you.
- I care about you.
- I feel your pain.
- You are not alone.
- I made you wonderfully.
- You are beloved and chosen.
- You are mine.
- I will mold you into my image and use this trial for your good.
- I will enable you to love and serve the family I have given to you.

As I consistently listen to the voice of my Good Shepherd and not my flesh, the devil, or the lies of the world, I found peace and healing for my soul. I was able to smile at my future because Jesus was with me (Proverbs 31:25).

Jesus is with you too, dear friend. Bring your troublesome thoughts to Him, and He will speak Truth to you, quiet your mind, and bring rest to your soul. There is thought-taming grace for you.

Question 7: What are your final thoughts about today's lesson? Please share.

_____

_____

_____

_____

Intimacy
A Picture of Christ and the Church

*G*ood day, and welcome back to the A United Front course.

Are you ready for another lesson of rejoicing in the gospel and being empowered to walk in the Truth of it? I hope that you are.

Today we are addressing the issue of physical intimacy—sex—in a gospel-centered marriage.

> *I will not be addressing the how-to aspects of this topic. There are many good books written from a Christian perspective, which can inspire you and answer questions related to sexual intercourse.*

Physical intimacy in marriage was designed to model the relationship between Christ and His Bride.

> **Question 1:** Fill in the blank. *"Therefore, a man shall leave his father and mother and hold fast to his wife, and the _____ shall become _____ _____." This _____ is profound, and I am saying that it _____ to _____ and the _____. Ephesians 5:31-32*

Dear friend, don't miss this important point. Sex between a husband and wife is a physical illustration of a spiritual reality.

Think about it, a husband removes his clothing, enters his wife and, after some physical effort, releases to her that which gives life, pleasure, and satisfaction. Similarly, Christ removed His royal robes of righteousness, stepped down into our nakedness and poured out His very life (Matthew 26:27-28) to bring us into eternal life (John 3:16) and make us full and complete. *"For in Christ all the fullness of the Deity lives in bodily form, and in Christ you have been brought to fullness"* (Colossians 2:9-10). He alone can satisfy our souls now and eternally (Psalm 107:9). *In Him are pleasures forevermore* (Psalm 16:11)!

> **Question 2:** Have you ever viewed physical intimacy within marriage in this way? Please share.
>
> _____
>
> _____
>
> _____

Growing up, I somehow missed this profound mystery. As a child, sex was not discussed with me except in hushed and stern tones in which I was told that I was not to do it. Never mind that I didn't know what "it" was. Because of my ignorance, individuals took liberties with my body that they should not have. I was repeatedly molested as a child and young teen and raped as a young adult.

My experiences both confused and distressed me. As I aged, I began to see sex as a tool—a way to get the attention and approval I craved. And then sex became a duty—a marital responsibility. Eventually, sex became associated with shame when I understood and felt the effects of immorality that had marred my life, mind, body, and marital bed.

I had a distorted view of sex because I had allowed the world, my flesh, and the devil to inform my mind instead of Christ and His cross.

Question 3: Have you been viewing, or have you ever viewed sexual intimacy from a worldly point of view? Please share.

_____

_____

_____

_____

In the beginning, Adam and Eve were naked and unashamed (Genesis 2:24-25), but after they sinned, everything changed (Genesis 3): pain, anguish, division, shame, and fear all marred every aspect of human life. And while we have never known the innocence of our first parents, we all understand the realities and destruction of sin.

Sexual impurity was a blight on my marriage; it was a plague of pain, frustration, and fear that afflicted my husband and me and left us clinging to life. After the sexual impurity in our marriage came to light, sex in our marriage was a bit awkward. I was afraid because I feared my husband was not attracted to me. My husband wrestled with shame and guilt. We were a mess.

Question 4: Has sexual impurity marred your view of sex with your spouse? Please explain.

_____

_____

_____

_____

This struggle of sexual impurity is a common one which has plagued the Church from the beginning. Specifically, the Church in Corinth struggled in this area, and so, Paul wrote to them about it.

In 1 Corinthians 5, Paul makes it clear that sexual immorality in the life of the believer is something to be mourned. He goes further and reinforces these truths in chapter 6: "_The body is not meant for sexual immorality, but for_ *the Lord, and the Lord for the body. And God raised the Lord and will also raise us up by his power...Or do you not know that your body is a temple of the Holy Spirit within you, whom you have from God? You are not your own, for you were bought with a price. So, glorify God in your body." 1 Corinthians 6:13b-14; 19-20*

Question 5: According to 1 Corinthians 6, for what were our bodies meant?
- ☐ For the Lord
- ☐ For hard work
- ☐ For sexual immorality

Our bodies are for the Lord and His glory. And we want to glorify God in our bodies, minds, and marriages. But the question comes - how? Hasn't sin ruined everything? What should we do? The Corinthians had similar questions, and we read the answers in 1 Corinthians 7.

"Now concerning the matters about which you wrote: "It is good for a man not to have sexual relations with a woman." But because of the temptation to sexual immorality, each man should have his own wife and each woman her own husband. The husband should give to his wife her conjugal rights, and likewise the wife to her husband. For the wife does not have authority over her own body, but the husband does. Likewise, the husband does not have authority over his own body, but the wife does. Do not deprive one another, except perhaps by agreement for a limited time, that you may devote yourselves to prayer; but then come together again so that Satan may not tempt you because of your lack of self-control." 1 Corinthians 7: 1-5

Question 6: Because of the temptation toward sexual impurity, what means of grace does 1 Corinthians 7:2 teach?
- ☐ Cold Showers
- ☐ Exercise
- ☐ Marriage

It seems that the Corinthians had asked Paul if it would be better to totally withdraw from sexual activity and be entirely devoted to the Lord. Abstinence is a common response to sexual impurity.

Indeed, I have repeatedly heard variations of the following: "I don't want my spouse to fantasize about other people while he/she is intimate with me, so there will be no sex until I know my spouse's mind is pure."

The primary problem with this approach is that it is not a gospel response to sexual impurity which the subsequent verses in 1 Corinthians 7 prove. The secondary problem is there is no way for you ever to be sure of what is in the mind of your spouse.

Abstinence is not the answer; sex within marriage is God's answer to sexual temptation. Physical intimacy between a husband and wife is a means of grace to help fend off the enticements of sexual impurity.

We must accept that we live in an immoral world, in bodies of flesh; temptations will come to us all. Being a Christian does not insulate us from temptation; in fact, as children of God, we are of more interest to the devil than unbelievers.

For this reason, it is an absolute necessity for us to be centered in the gospel of Jesus Christ. Our enemy, the devil, is roaming about seeking whom he may devour (1 Peter 5:8); and we cannot overcome the evil one apart from the power of the gospel. We must stand firm in the gospel and not neglect God's means of sustaining grace, dear friend; or else we risk our marriages being torn apart as those who have no hope. *"Do not deprive one another, except perhaps by agreement for a limited time, that you may devote yourselves to prayer; but then come together again so that Satan may not tempt you because of your lack of self-control." 1 Corinthians 7:5*

According to 1 Corinthians 7:5, there are the three conditions given for refraining from sexual intimacy in marriage. They are:

1. It should be by mutual agreement
2. It is only for a limited time
3. It is so that you may devote yourselves to prayer (some translations add "and fasting").

This instruction is not a small or casual suggestion given as a way to avoid sex. Paul makes this recommendation because sexual impurity is a powerful and destructive lure of the devil.

Friend, you cannot fight against the dark and demonic forces of sexual sin with physical weapons or in your own power (Ephesians 6:10-18). If you want to win this war, you must unite together with your spouse and fight this battle kneeling at the foot of the cross of Christ.

Coming together as a couple to seek the Lord in prayer for the healing of your marriage is not only a fulfilling and uniting experience, but it is a powerful battle strategy.

If you and your spouse elect to abstain from sex for prayer, you might also consider adding the fasting from food component. Going without food for a time heightens our awareness of our desperate need for God and His power, and it can add intensity and passion to our prayers that might otherwise be lacking. It also helps to remind us that sexual separation is to be temporary, even as fasting from food cannot be permanent. Let the fasting turn into feasting once you come together in physical intimacy again.

Also, it is essential to define the "limited time" before you begin. Set a date, put it on the calendar, and plan a special time of lovemaking to celebrate the anticipated answer to your prayers.

> **Question 7:** How can physical intimacy in marriage help you fight against the attacks of sexual impurity on your marriage?
>
> _____
>
> _____
>
> _____
>
> _____

We began this lesson by exploring the connection between physical intimacy in marriage and the intimacy between Christ and His Bride (the Church). The oneness between Christ and His Bride is beautiful and made possible by Christ's death on the cross.

Sexual impurity has brought shame and sorrow into our homes, but Christ is greater, and He has overcome for us. By His wounds, our marriages are healed (1 Peter 2:24). On the cross, Christ bore our sins, carried our sorrows, removed our shame and disgrace and wrapped us up in His beautiful white robes of righteousness.

His perfect love casts out our fear and enables us to be physically intimate with our spouse, joyful in the knowledge that our union illustrates the perfect and eternal union we will all experience someday at the consummation of all things, the "marriage supper of the Lamb" (Revelation 19:7-10).

I pray that you see sexual intimacy in marriage as the means of grace that it is and that you are rejoicing in Jesus and this physical reminder of His perfect love.

Physical Intimacy
Joy and Pleasure

*H*ello and welcome back to the A United Front course.

In lesson 25, we addressed the issue of physical intimacy in a gospel-centered marriage. We reminded ourselves that sex within marriage is a physical illustration of a spiritual reality—the complete oneness of Christ and the Church. We understand the grace of physical intimacy in marriage for warding off the temptations of sexual immorality, and we rejoiced in the restorative power of the gospel.

Today, we will focus on the biblical description of pleasure within marital intimacy. This topic is important because the temptation exists to merely go through the motions of sex to fulfill our marital duty. But to have this kind of attitude is to rob ourselves of a gift God intended for us to enjoy.

The same is true for those who go through the motions of Christian faith without having any pleasure in Jesus. Friend, doing this (going through the motions) is religion; doing our religious duty yet without any joy in the relationship. *And it is vital to know that Jesus came not to give us a religion but a fulfilling and loving relationship* with Himself (John 10:10).

Notice the deep intimacy of Jesus' prayer for His people in John 17: *"The glory that you have given me I have given to them, that they may be one even as we are one, I in them and you in me, that they may become perfectly one, so that the world may know that you sent me and loved them even as you loved me." John 17:22-23*

This deep intimacy amongst the Trinity and between Christ and His bride is what sex between a husband and wife illustrates for us. To miss this point is to rob ourselves of both a great understanding and a great experience within marriage.

The book of Song of Solomon is a precious book about the lover and His beloved. It is a very sensual book which uses the physical story of the lover and his beloved to illustrate the deeply intimate and passionate relationship between Christ and His Bride. We will briefly consider some passages from this book, so that we might understand more about God's design for sex within marriage, which is not merely to procreate, not only to picture Christ and the church, but also to provide pleasure to both people.

Let's begin.

> "Let him kiss me with the kisses of his mouth! For your love is better than wine; your anointing oils are fragrant; your name is oil poured out; therefore, virgins love you. Draw me after you; let us run. The king has brought me into his chambers." Song of Solomon 1: 1-4

Question 1: In Song of Solomon 1:1-4, the bride joyfully sings about her lover. What does the bride want her groom to do?
- ☐ She wants the groom to pour her wine.
- ☐ She wants her groom to kiss her and to be intimate with her.
- ☐ She wants her groom to go for a run.

From the start, we can see that the bride desires physical intimacy with her lover. The bride wants to be kissed and taken into the bedchamber – his love is more intoxicating than wine to her. She reaches out for the pleasure that her lover can bring to her. This is good and right. Even the friends encourage this mindset of pursuing pleasure in love when they say to the couple, *"drink your fill of love."* Song of Solomon 5:1

Question 2: Where are you with sexual desire for your spouse?

_____

_____

_____

_____

　　　SETTING CAPTIVES FREE

Perhaps when you were first married, you felt desire for your spouse, but now sin and betrayal have clouded your viewpoint, and you no longer see anything desirable about your spouse. Or maybe you are like me, I desired my husband, but he used to reject my sexual advances, which was deeply wounding.

It is true, sin destroys, but we must remember that Jesus saves and restores. Through His death on the cross and His resurrection, He brings love, forgiveness, grace, and healing, where it is needed (Mark 2:17)! Where sin ruins, Jesus restores. Where sin kills, Jesus brings new life.

Indeed, we can find healing for our hearts and gospel empowering strength in Christ's love. Jesus kisses us with a thousand kisses of pardon every day. He loves us and covers our sin with His precious blood. There is nothing more intoxicating than His love for us—His perfect, everlasting, unfailing, always faithful, never wavering love—which He displayed so vividly by stretching His arms wide and dying on the cross in our place. And this incredible, exquisite love has been poured into our hearts through His Holy Spirit which He has given to us as a Comforter (Romans 5:5; John 14:16). His name is music to our ears, comfort to our minds, and peace to our souls. He is Jesus—our Lover and our Beloved.

Question 3: Do you feel Christ's love for you; do you desire Him? Please share.

_____

_____

_____

_____

Oh, friend, Jesus has called you into a relationship with Him for His joy and yours (Psalm 37:4)! He wants you to find pleasure in Him, for when you do, you will say with the bride, *"Behold, you are beautiful, my beloved, truly delightful." Song of Solomon 1:16*

We must delight ourselves in the Lord because as we do, we are enabled to forgive and again enjoy physical intimacy in marriage.

If we believe in the resurrection, then we must believe it in a way that permeates to every area of life. When Jesus rose from the dead, He was not a ghost or the shell of a person. He was fully alive – able to be touched, to eat, to speak, to be seen. Similarly, when the gospel touches our marriages, they are raised from the dead, healed and restored, not in part but wholly.

You must not deny yourself the delight of physical intimacy in your marriage because to refuse intimacy with your repentant spouse is to deny the healing and restorative power of the gospel.

The joy of physical intimacy in marriage is comparable to the believer's joy in Jesus Christ, who having not seen, yet we love and *rejoice in Him "with joy unspeakable and full of glory"* (1 Peter 1:8). This is the same joy that we spouses can get a taste of on this earth, during physical intimacy, if we will seek for it.

Question 4: How can experiencing joy in Christ and His gospel help restore the pleasure of sexual intimacy in your marriage?

_____

_____

_____

_____

Sadly, some might be tempted to say "my spouse is not at all like the bride or groom of Song of Solomon. Sure, I would find joy in intimacy if he/she were all these things, but mine is not so I cannot. My spouse has been impure and has destroyed any hope for sexual pleasure in our marriage." Oh, how sad to let the devil win like this, and to refuse to live as *"more than conquerors through Him Who loved us"* (Romans 8:37) by reclaiming joy in intimacy.

Friend, because of Jesus' death on the cross and His victorious resurrection, sin can be forgiven, relationships reconciled, and joy restored in intimacy. My husband and I are living proof, and we are just one couple amongst thousands who have found forgiveness and restoration in Christ. You can, too, but you must look past the sin of your spouse to see the Savior.

As we finish up our lesson, please read these passages from Song of Solomon that display the pleasure of sexual love in marriage.

As an apple tree among the trees of the forest, so is my beloved among the young men. With great delight I sat in his shadow, and his fruit was sweet to my taste. He brought me to the banqueting house, and his banner over me was love. Sustain me with raisins; refresh me with apples, for I am sick with love. Song of Songs 2:3-5

My beloved is mine, and I am his; he grazes among the lilies. Song of Songs 2:16

His mouth is most sweet, and he is altogether desirable. This is my beloved and this is my friend, O daughters of Jerusalem. Song of Songs 5:16

Question 5: Select one of the passages above or any passage from Song of Solomon and rewrite it in your own words as you might speak it to your spouse.

_____

_____

_____

_____

I do hope you are finding your soul stirred by our pleasing theme ("My heart overflows with a pleasing theme" *Psalm 45: 1a*), and that your understanding of the biblical pleasure within sexual intimacy is growing.

But if you find that you don't identify with pleasure in physical intimacy with your spouse yet, I urge you to pour out your heart before the Lord. He can restore what sin has damaged.

Unspeakable joy in sexual intimacy is the biblical example and is what God calls you to pursue in your sexual relationship with your spouse.

Friend, as we draw near to Christ and feast on His love, our view of all things—ourselves, our husbands, our marriage, and even sex—is transformed.

When we focus on the sins committed against us, we see only the ugly, the pain, rejection, and the negative aspects of our husbands and our lives. But as we fellowship with Jesus and sit at his feet, we find our sight transformed by the good news of what Jesus has done and will do for us. Where once we saw the sins against us, now we see the forgiveness and grace of Jesus shining gloriously. Where once we saw the agony of defeat and the stink of death, now we see the joys of victory and the pleasing aroma of new life in Christ.

> **Question 6:** Does the gospel change your view of your husband, your marriage, and sex? Please share.

_____

_____

_____

_____

The death and resurrection of Jesus should not only change the way we view sexual intimacy in our marriages, but it should also empower us to *enjoy* the gift of sex that God has given to us.

Tomorrow, we will finish this section on physical intimacy by looking at how the bride pursues her lover, and we will discover that this is a wondrous and loving art in itself.

Physical Intimacy
Captivated by Love

*H*ello, and welcome. I pray that you are finding this study beneficial and worth the time and effort you have invested.

For the past two lessons, we have been discussing physical intimacy in a gospel-centered marriage. We saw that physical intimacy is an illustration of the spiritual union between Christ and the church. We've discussed the significance of enjoying sexual relations with our spouse because it brings God glory when we delight in the gift He has given us. And now we will finish up our study of physical intimacy with a lesson on the benefits of drawing our spouse to us.

From the beginning, the devil has done his best to seduce God's people into sin. For everything beautiful that God has given to us for our good and our enjoyment, the devil has offered a counterfeit and destructive version. This is especially true in the area of sex where Satan offers pornography and sexual immorality to lure people away from the spouse God has given. But the devil does this in every area of life, and all of us are susceptible to his seductions.

Question 1: Has the devil ever seduced you with anything? What happened? Please share.

_____

_____

_____

_____

Over the years, the devil has seduced me with many cunning lies. Just as he promised Eve that she would be like God if she ate of the forbidden fruit, so Satan told me that if I just asserted myself and demanded better treatment, then I would be happy. And just like Eve, I was deceived (2 Corinthians 11:3) so I put my foot down in anger and gave ultimatums; but instead of better treatment, I gained alienation. My aggressive behavior only pushed my husband away from me; it did not achieve the righteous life that God desires for my husband or me. *"Know this, my beloved brothers: let every person be quick to hear, slow to speak, slow to anger; for the anger of man does not produce the righteousness of God."* James 1:19-20

Thankfully, God showed me the error of my ways and brought me to repentance. Now I am quite content to leave the disciplinary actions to God (Romans 12:19).

Regarding sexual fulfillment, the devil promises our spouses that they will get more enjoyment and satisfaction away from us. Look with me at Proverbs 7:10-22 to see how the seduction unfolds.

> *"And behold, the woman meets him, dressed as a prostitute, wily of heart...now in the street, now in the market, and at every corner she lies in wait. She seizes him and kisses him...so now I have come out to meet you, to seek you eagerly, and I have found you. I have spread my couch with coverings, colored linens from Egyptian linen; I have perfumed my bed with myrrh, aloes, and cinnamon. Come, let us take our fill of love till morning; let us delight ourselves with love...With much seductive speech she persuades him; with her smooth talk she compels him. All at once he follows her..."*

Question 2: According to Proverbs 7, where does the seduction happen? Fill in the blank. *"now in the _____, now in the _____, and at _____ _____she lies in wait."*

Do you see how relentless the devil's seduction is? The adulteress worked hard at getting the man into her bed. She was everywhere, appealing to his eyes by dressing seductively. She aroused his body by touching and kissing him. She lured his ego by making him feel important with her words. She appealed to his senses with perfume, soft sheets, and a place prepared especially for him. And finally, she gave him time, all night long. And while her seduction is impressive and alluring upfront, we know that it leads to death (Proverbs 7:23).

The interesting thing about the adulteress woman is that what she does is only wrong because she does it with someone who is not her husband. And such is the devil's way. He takes something beautiful (sexual attractiveness) and perverts it by directing it toward someone who is not the spouse.

We do not want to be like Adam, sitting back and allowing the evil one to seduce our spouse without interruption (Genesis 3). There is a right and God-glorifying way for our spouses to be stimulated sexually, which leads to joy and delight. And it is this way, this godly drawing, or enticement, which we will discuss for the rest of this lesson.

> **Question 3:** What was the problem with the sexual seduction in Proverbs 7:10-22?
> ☐ The woman was seductive
> ☐ The woman was seducing someone who was not her spouse.
> ☐ The woman was spending too much money

Sometimes in our zeal to abstain from every form of evil, we can forget to hold fast to that which is good (I Thessalonians 5:21-22).

I've met people who believe that sex is not meant to be enjoyed but only endured for procreation, but the Bible says otherwise. We saw from our study of Song of Solomon; God encourages couples to enjoy each other sexually.

In Proverbs 5:18-19 the instruction is given, *"Let your fountain be blessed, and rejoice in the wife of your youth, a lovely deer, a graceful doe. Let her breasts fill you at all times with delight; be intoxicated always in her love."*

> **Question 4:** In Proverbs 5:18-19, what are we instructed to do?
> ☐ Rejoice in our spouse, delight in their body, and be intoxicated by their love.
> ☐ Rejoice in our home, delight in our children, and be intoxicated by wine.
> ☐ Rejoice in our life, delight in our food, and be intoxicated by laughter.

Now perhaps you are thinking, "That's right. My spouse shouldn't have gone off into immorality; he/she was supposed to come to me and find satisfaction in me." True, but, dear friend, remember the power and relentlessness of the devil's seduction. We must not forget the times we have fallen prey to the devil's traps. I urge you toward cross-centered love and Christ-like compassion.

Do not lay blame, but instead seek to *restore* and *reclaim* what is rightfully yours. And I'm not just talking about your spouse. I'm speaking of *your sexuality and your powers of attraction.*

If your spouse is to find satisfaction in your body, then you must not only be available but also alluring. You don't put a supermarket bag of uncooked food items on the table for dinner and expect everyone to eat it up. It takes a little time to cook and prepare meals, but it is time well invested. How much *more* valuable is the time you take to prepare yourself for your spouse.

Now to be clear, I am speaking of more than lighting a candle and putting on some nice music once a month. If you want your spouse to be captivated and intoxicated by your love, then you must learn what captivates him/her.

You want to appeal to all the senses, sight, taste, smell, touch, and hearing, so ask yourself these questions:

- How does your spouse like you to dress?
- Do they comment on your attractiveness in a specific color or style of clothing?
- Do they prefer one scent over another?
- What words can you use to build up and attract your spouse?
- What kind of touch does your spouse enjoy?
- Is your bedroom a welcoming and romantic space?

Listen to your spouse, learn and share your own preferences. Then work together to merge your likings for a mutually enjoyable experience.

It is crucial that you do not reject your spouse's sexual advances. "*The husband should fulfill his marital duty to his wife, and likewise the wife to her husband. The wife's body does not belong to her alone but also to her husband. In the same way, the husband's body does not belong to him alone but also to his wife. Do not deprive each other except by mutual consent and for a time, so that you may devote yourselves to prayer. Then come together again so that Satan will not tempt you because of your lack of self-control." 1 Corinthians 7:3-5 (NIV)*

If you have rejected your spouse's advances in the past, then apologize. Tell them that you realize that what you did was wrong and that from now on you will make every effort to receive him/her with joy. This does not mean that you will have sexual intercourse immediately upon request (though spontaneous sex is fun), but it does mean that you will not reject your spouse.

For example, your spouse comes to you while you are cleaning the kitchen, embraces you, and invites you for sexual intimacy. If possible, go—the dishes can wait. If you can't go immediately, receive your spouse by responding affectionately and ask if you can meet up in "X" number of minutes (something realistic). And if full intercourse isn't an option for you, be sure to offer an alternative such as manual stimulation. Take the opportunity to use your God-given imagination to show love to your spouse and enjoy them at the same time.

If you are struggling in this area of life, I invite you to come to Jesus and remember how you have been loved and received unwaveringly by Him. Jesus said, *"...whoever comes to me I will never drive away."* John 6:37 NIV

While you were still a sinner and undeserving of any love, Jesus loved you and laid down His life for you on the cross. When you sin, Jesus does not reject you, He calls you to return to Him and receive His love again. Friend, this how we should be with our spouses. When your spouse repents, forgive them and invite them back into your love.

Question 5: Why is it important that you not reject your spouse's sexual advances?

_____

_____

_____

_____

Physical intimacy within marriage is unique to the couple. There is no "one size fits all," which is why I have avoided specifics regarding frequency or style, but there are biblical principles given for guidance such as being available to our spouse and learning how to love them in a captivating way.

In closing, I want to show you that not only is enticing your spouse a wise and beautiful thing to do, but the concept is also rooted in the gospel.

> *You are altogether beautiful, my love; there is no flaw in you. Come with me from Lebanon, my bride; come with me from Lebanon. Depart from the peak of Amana, from the peak of Senir and Hermon, from the dens of lions, from the mountains of leopards. You have captivated my heart, my sister, my bride; you have captivated my heart with one glance of your eyes, with one jewel of your necklace. How beautiful is your love, my sister, my bride! How much better is your love than wine and the fragrance of your oils than any spice! Your lips drip nectar, my bride; honey and milk are under your tongue; the fragrance of your garments is like the fragrance of Lebanon. Song of Solomon 4:7-11*

King Solomon speaks these eloquent words to his bride, but they also express the heart of our eternal Bridegroom to us.

Jesus says to us, *"You are beautiful; there is no flaw in you."* And why can He say this? Because His blood has washed us clean (Ephesians 5:2-27). He is captivated with us and intoxicated by the love which He has poured into our hearts. (Romans 5:5)

The gospel of Jesus restores the marriage bed and makes it a place of enjoyment and delight. When you love your spouse and draw them sexually, you are modeling the profound mystery of Christ and His Bride.

Question 6: Does the gospel change your view of sexual intimacy and the drawing of your husband?

_____

_____

_____

_____

Rejoicing in the Gospel

*G*reetings and welcome back. I am happy and thankful that you are here.

Anytime sexual impurity touches a marriage, the temptation exists to allow the sin and the pain of the moment to steal away the joy of our salvation. If we succumb to the temptation, we will become focused on our problems, and this leads to depression, anger, fear, and bitterness. But God, who is rich in mercy, has provided a way out of this trap, and that's what our lesson is about today.

Let's begin this study with the words Paul wrote to the persecuted church in Thessalonica: *"Rejoice always, pray without ceasing, give thanks in all circumstances; for this is the will of God in Christ Jesus for you." 1 Thessalonians 5:16-18*

Question 1: According to 1 Thessalonians 5:16-18, what is the will of God for you:
- ☐ To rejoice, pray, and give thanks in all circumstances.
- ☐ To sing, dance, and be happy.
- ☐ To laugh, live, and have a good time.

It is God's will for us to rejoice, pray and give thanks in all things. And these instructions aren't merely a suggestion for our consideration, they are commands.

It is interesting to note that these words were written by Paul who faced some harsh circumstances. Take a moment and consider this description of Paul's life that he shared in his letter to the Corinthians:

"Five times I received at the hands of the Jews the forty lashes less one. Three times I was beaten with rods. Once I was stoned. Three times I was shipwrecked; a night and a day I was adrift at sea;

on frequent journeys, in danger from rivers, danger from robbers, danger from my own people, danger from Gentiles, danger in the city, danger in the wilderness, danger at sea, danger from false brothers; in toil and hardship, through many a sleepless night, in hunger and thirst, often without food, in cold and exposure. And, apart from other things, there is the daily pressure on me of my anxiety for all the churches." 2 Corinthians 11:24-28

Paul didn't write these words, "rejoice, pray and give thanks in all things" to the persecuted believers in Thessalonica flippantly. No, he was well acquainted with suffering. And God used all these dreadful experiences to teach Paul the power of rejoicing, praying, and giving thanks.

When considering these commands, we must first take note of the object of our rejoicing. Look with me at Philippians 4:4, *"Rejoice in the Lord always; again, I will say, rejoice."* Again, we see the command to rejoice always, but this time, the instruction is more specific.

> **Question 2:** According to Philippians 4:4, in Whom are we to rejoice always?
> ☐ In ourselves.
> ☐ In the Church.
> ☐ In the Lord.

Indeed, the whole world can be falling down around us (and sometimes it is), but there is always a reason to rejoice in Jesus.

God isn't commanding us to be happy that we are going through hardship. He isn't saying, "I've given you what's good for you, and you'd better be grateful for it" like a stern parent making us swallow cod liver oil and say, "Thank you."

No! God loved us so much that He sent His one and only Son Jesus down to us. God Himself entered into our humanity and became subject to all the weaknesses of our flesh. He now can sympathize with our weaknesses (Hebrews 4:15) and identify with our struggles and sufferings.

And not only that, but He also carried our sorrows and our grief (Isaiah 53: 3-4). He went to the cross, became sin for us to give us His righteousness (2 Corinthians 5: 21). Then He rose from the dead to justify us before God. Our sin was fully paid for, and the resurrection of Jesus shows that God accepted Jesus' sacrifice as payment in full. Now all who believe are justified from all sin. *"Through Him, everyone who believes is justified from everything you could not be justified from by the law of Moses" (Acts 13:39 BSB).*

Today God looks at every believer through the righteousness of Jesus, and He sees you as *"holy in his sight, without blemish, and free from accusation"* (Colossians 1:22b NIV). God sees you as perfect and holy as Jesus Christ Himself is. You, as a believer, are wearing His righteousness as a robe, and therefore, are accepted by God. *"I delight greatly in the Lord; my soul rejoices in my God. For He has clothed me with the garments of salvation and arrayed me in a robe of righteousness..." (Isaiah 61:10 NIV).*

Jesus did all this for us because He loves us. He calls us to rejoice in Him, pray to Him and give thanks to Him because He loves us; and He knows this is the only way we can navigate the storms of this life safely.

These commands—rejoice in the Lord, pray without ceasing, and give thanks in all things—are God calling us to be with Him.

God calls to you today as if He were saying, "Come to Me. In Me, you will find salvation, a reason for joy and gratitude, a listening ear, a loving heart, a kind and encouraging word, and sustaining power."

Question 3: Are you rejoicing in the Lord today? Please share.

_____

_____

_____

_____

Much as Peter began to sink beneath the waves when he took His eyes off Jesus (Matthew 14: 28-32), so we too begin to lose heart and sink beneath our circumstances when we look away from the cross of Jesus.

It might seem impossible to rejoice in the Lord when your heart has been wounded by your spouse, but the key to rejoicing and giving thanks in all things is to look to Jesus. Look at His eyes full of love for you. Look at His hands and remember that He was pierced for your transgressions (Isaiah

53:5). Look at His radiant face, remembering the promise for every believer, *they will see his face* (Revelation 22:4). Look at His suffering in your place. Look at His death and resurrection. Look at how He is interceding for you. Fix your eyes on Jesus (Hebrews 12:2-3), and you will be able to rejoice and give thanks in all things.

Now, not only are these commands—rejoicing, praying and giving thanks as we contemplate Christ—a way for us to walk above our difficult circumstances without sinking, but they are also powerful tools against the evil one.

Look with me now to *Acts 16:19-25*, *"But when her owners saw that their hope of gain was gone, they seized Paul and Silas and dragged them into the marketplace before the rulers. And when they had brought them to the magistrates, they said, "These men are Jews, and they are disturbing our city. They advocate customs that are not lawful for us as Romans to accept or practice." The crowd joined in attacking them, and the magistrates tore the garments off them and gave orders to beat them with rods. And when they had inflicted many blows upon them, they threw them into prison, ordering the jailer to keep them safely. Having received this order, he put them into the inner prison and fastened their feet in the stocks. About midnight Paul and Silas were praying and singing hymns to God, and the prisoners were listening to them, and suddenly there was a great earthquake, so that the foundations of the prison were shaken. And immediately all the doors were opened, and everyone's bonds were unfastened."*

> **Question 4:** Paul and Silas were beaten and imprisoned for preaching the gospel and casting a demon out of a young girl. According to Acts 16:25, what were Paul and Silas doing during their imprisonment?
> - ☐ Telling everyone how unfair it was for them to be in prison.
> - ☐ Tending to their wounds and feeling sorry for themselves.
> - ☐ Praying and singing hymns to God.

Paul and Silas had been beaten and locked down for the night; and instead of railing about the injustice of it all, they were praying and singing hymns to God! In response, God sent an earthquake and set them free.

When we call upon the Almighty, rejoice in Him, and give thanks to Him, we should expect the miraculous. Our God is mighty to save! No situation is so dark and challenging that the Light of our Savior cannot penetrate it.

But wait, there is more! Read with me the rest of the story.

> Acts 16:27-34, *"When the jailer woke and saw that the prison doors were open, he drew his sword and was about to kill himself, supposing that the prisoners had escaped. But Paul cried with a loud voice, "Do not harm yourself, for we are all here." And the jailer called for lights and rushed in and trembling with fear he fell down before Paul and Silas. Then he brought them out and said, "Sirs, what must I do to be saved?" And they said, "Believe in the Lord Jesus, and you will be saved, you and your household." And they spoke the word of the Lord to him and to all who were in his house. And he took them the same hour of the night and washed their wounds; and he was baptized at once, he and all his family. Then he brought them up into his house and set food before them. And he rejoiced along with his entire household that he had believed in God."*

Question 5: According to Acts 16:30, how does the jailer respond to everything that has happened?
- ☐ He took his family and ran away in fear.
- ☐ He and his household believed in Jesus and were baptized that very night.
- ☐ He put everyone back in jail and locked the door.

The jailer became a Christian; in fact, the jailer's whole household was saved. Paul and Silas went from being beaten and in chains to clean, comforted and clothed, and rejoicing with a house of new converts; all this in just a matter of hours.

Rejoicing in God, praying, and giving thanks is evangelistic. When we face difficulties in this life, and we respond with joy in the Lord, hope-filled prayers, and a thankful heart, those around us will take notice, including your spouse. And you might even get to see the person (or people) who harmed you come to faith in Christ.

Question 6: How can your rejoicing, praying and giving thanks in all things invite others to put their faith in Christ?

_____

_____

_____

_____

Dear friend, whatever your circumstances (repentant spouse or not), if you are in Christ, you have a reason to rejoice. You have a Savior Who gave His life for you, a resurrected Lord Who has promised to lead you, a God who hears your prayers; you have every reason to give thanks! I pray that God will enable a thankful and rejoicing heart in us today. You are loved!

Comforted and Comforting

*H*ello and welcome back to the A United Front course. As you have completed the lessons in this course, it has been my prayer that you would find hope and comfort in the gospel of our Lord Jesus Christ as well as help in becoming a united front with your spouse.

In Matthew 5:4, speaking to His disciples, Jesus said, *"Blessed are those who mourn, for they will be comforted."* And He follows this with the promise that when He left, He would send another Comforter to be with and in His people (John 14:16-17 KJV) - the Holy Spirit.

For today's lesson, we will delve into what it means to be comforted by God and how those who are comforted respond. Let's begin by considering *2 Corinthians 1:3-5, "Blessed be the God and Father of our Lord Jesus Christ, the Father of mercies and God of all comfort, who comforts us in all our affliction, so that we may be able to comfort those who are in any affliction, with the comfort with which we ourselves are comforted by God. For as we share abundantly in Christ's sufferings, so through Christ, we share abundantly in comfort too."*

> **Question 1:** According to 2 Corinthians 1:3-5, who comforts us and why does He do it?
> ☐ God comforts us so that we may comfort others.
> ☐ The church comforts us so that we will be happy.
> ☐ God comforts us so that we will stop complaining.

Paul speaks to the Corinthians in praise to God, who comforts us so that we may be able to comfort others with the comfort we've received in Jesus. Notice how we share in Christ's sufferings and how that through Christ, we share in His consolation. Primarily, we find comfort in the message of the cross, the love Jesus poured out to forgive us and set us free. Like the beggars who shared their bread and riches (2 Kings 7:3-10), we share the powerful message of Jesus Christ and Him crucified with others to provide them with the same comfort we've received in Christ at the foot of the cross.

So that we can be confident in the message of comfort we have received, let's pause and remind ourselves by reading some passages from Isaiah 53.

> *"He was despised and rejected by men; a man of sorrows, and acquainted with grief, and as one from whom men hide their faces, he was despised, and we esteemed him not. Surely, he has borne our griefs and carried our sorrows; yet we esteemed him stricken, smitten by God, and afflicted." Isaiah 53:3-4*

To comfort us and relieve our distress, our Jesus suffered being despised and rejected by man. He carried our griefs (anxieties, diseases) and our sorrows (anguish, pain) (Philippians 4:4). He was struck repeatedly with fists and whips, and even worse, He was smitten by God, stricken by Him and afflicted.

My heart aches with gratitude to consider how our perfect and innocent Lord endured all this so that we might be accepted, welcomed, and received with pleasure by the Father (Ephesians 1:6). We can cast our cares and anxieties on Christ (1 Peter 5:7) and know joy even in the worst circumstances because Jesus has borne our griefs and carried our sorrows. Jesus received and drank all the cup of God's wrath against sin so that we could drink the cup of freedom. What a relief to know that we, as believers, will never be without hope because our hope is anchored to Christ and His finished work on the cross (Hebrews 6:19). What a comfort!

> *"But he was pierced for our transgressions; he was crushed for our iniquities; upon him was the chastisement that brought us peace, and with his wounds we are healed. All we like sheep have gone astray; we have turned—everyone—to his own way; and the LORD has laid on him the iniquity of us all. He was oppressed, and he was afflicted, yet he opened not his mouth; like a lamb that is led to the slaughter, and like a sheep that before its shearers is silent, so he opened not his mouth." Isaiah 53:5-7*

Question 2: Which one of Christ's sufferings from Isaiah 53:5-7 stands out the most to you and why?

_____

_____

_____

_____

I'm greatly comforted by the words, *"the Lord laid on Him the iniquity of us all."*

All my sins, your sins, the sins of the whole world (1 John 2:2) were laid on Christ at the cross. Those sins can *never be attached to us because God put them on Jesus!* Our sins were nailed to a tree and buried in a tomb; we bear them no more; now, we can sing, *"It is well with my soul!"*

Jesus was pierced through the heart to provide healing for our hearts. He was led like a lamb to the slaughter into utter agony so that His Holy Spirit might lead us into peace, love, joy, patience, goodness, and self-control. Oh, what good news and comfort for a weary and hurting heart.

> Isaiah 53:10-12, *"Yet it was the will of the LORD to crush him; he has put him to grief; when his soul makes an offering for guilt, he shall see his offspring; he shall prolong his days; the will of the LORD shall prosper in his hand. Out of the anguish of his soul he shall see and be satisfied; by his knowledge shall the righteous one, my servant, make many to be accounted righteous, and he shall bear their iniquities. Therefore I will divide him a portion with the many, and he shall divide the spoil with the strong, because he poured out his soul to death and was numbered with the transgressors; yet he bore the sin of many, and makes intercession for the transgressors."*

Question 3: According to Isaiah 53:12, what does Jesus do for sinners? Fill in the blank. *"yet he bore the sin of many and makes* _____ *for the* _____*."*

Not only does Jesus atone for your sins, but He also makes intercession for you! Oh, dear friend, be of good cheer! Jesus *"is able to save to the uttermost those who draw near to God through him, since he always lives to make intercession for them." (Hebrews 7:25)* In other words, you cannot be condemned for any past, present, or future sin because Jesus is ever pleading His blood for you. And the Father will not punish you because Jesus has already taken your punishment.

> **Question 4:** Are you comforted and cheered by what Christ has done for you on the cross and what He continues to do for you in heaven? Please share.
>
> _____
>
> _____
>
> _____
>
> _____

One of the best parts about finding our comfort at the cross is that it cannot be taken from us! Jesus cried out, *"It is finished!"* And indeed, it was. The book of Hebrews tells us that after He had atoned for our sins, Jesus sat down at the right hand of the Father (Hebrews 1:3; Hebrews 10:12). Considering all that Jesus has accomplished, we can say with Job, *"Though He slay me; I will hope in Him." (Job 13:15)* No matter how trying things in this life might be, those who believe in Jesus always have the comfort of His presence and His love. We have our eyes fixed not on our momentary troubles, but on that which is unseen and eternal (2 Corinthians 4:17-18).

Now that we have remembered the comfort we've received from God, let us return again to 2 Corinthians 1:3-4 and see the appropriate response: *"Blessed be the God and Father of our Lord Jesus Christ, the Father of mercies and God of all comfort, who comforts us in all our affliction, so that we may be able to comfort those who are in any affliction, with the comfort with which we ourselves are comforted by God."*

Question 5: According to 2 Corinthians 1:3-4, why does God comfort us? Fill in the blank. "...*who comforts us in all our affliction, so that* _____ _____ *be able to* _____ *those who are in any affliction...*"

God comforts us so that we will be able to comfort others who are in distress, not with our goodness but His. We are called and equipped to comfort others with this sweet and precious comfort we've received through Christ's death and resurrection. Please pray and ask God if He would want you to become a mentor with Setting Captives Free. Every day, hurting and broken-hearted people come to Setting Captives Free seeking hope and help in their time of need. As a mentor, you would use the message of reconciliation (2 Corinthians 5:18-19) to help these women by comforting them with the comfort you have received in Christ. Please write to helpdesk@settingcaptivesfree.com for more information on this ministry opportunity.

> *You need not have everything all figured out or resolved before you help others. Paul wrote to the Corinthians, "For what we proclaim is not ourselves, but Jesus Christ as Lord, with ourselves as your servants for Jesus' sake. For God, who said, "Let light shine out of darkness," has shone in our hearts to give the light of the knowledge of the glory of God in the face of Jesus Christ. But we have this treasure in jars of clay, to show that the surpassing power belongs to God and not to us. We are afflicted in every way, but not crushed; perplexed, but not driven to despair; persecuted, but not forsaken; struck down, but not destroyed; always carrying in the body the death of Jesus, so that the life of Jesus may also be manifested in our bodies." (2 Corinthians 4:5-10)*

We aren't proclaiming ourselves, but Christ and what He has done and can do. He is our Treasure and Comfort. He is the One to whom we point and encourage others to anchor their souls. We, ourselves, might be perplexed, persecuted or distressed, we are "jars of clay" (temporary, breakable), but we carry Jesus within us, and He is more than enough comfort and strength for all the hurting hearts there are.

Even if you decide not to become a mentor with Setting Captives Free, I pray that you will reach out to those who are local to you with loving arms of gospel comfort and hope whenever God gives you the opportunity.

Question 6: Will you pray about going on to become a mentor with the A United Front course?
- ☐ Yes
- ☐ No
- ☐ I have questions about this opportunity.

"So, if there is any encouragement in Christ, any comfort from love, any participation in the Spirit, any affection and sympathy, complete my joy by being of the same mind, having the same love, being in full accord and of one mind. Do nothing from selfish ambition or conceit, but in humility count others more significant than yourselves. Let each of you look not only to his own interests, but also to the interests of others." (Philippians 2:1-4)

May God enable us to look not only to our own interests but also to the interests of others in the days ahead; let us never withhold the comfort of the cross from anyone who is seeking it, especially our spouse.

Question 7: What are your final thoughts about this lesson? Do you have any questions? Please share.

_____

_____

_____

_____

In the next and final lesson, you will have the opportunity to share a testimony of what God has done in your heart and life. Please pray about what God would have you share. Your testimony of the transforming power of the gospel of Christ's atoning death and victorious resurrection and how it has brought healing to your heart might be the very word of hope and encouragement that another hurting spouse needs to hear.

Testimony

*H*ello friend, welcome to your final lesson in the A United Front course. In this lesson, you'll have an opportunity to share how God has worked in your heart and life during these past thirty lessons.

I have shared my experiences with you throughout this course, but here are some of the changes I experienced by God's grace after learning to live united with my husband in the shadow of the cross.

God has brought me into joyful intimacy with Jesus. Having fellowshipped with Christ in His sufferings, I enjoy a more intimate relationship with Him now *(Philippians 3:10)*.

My husband and I have much joy in spiritual, emotional, and physical intimacy and being united with Jesus Christ together. Christ has defeated the impurity that once threatened to destroy our marriage. We now share a close union walking by the Holy Spirit. "*A cord of three strands is not quickly broken.*" Ecclesiastes 4:12

I've been set free from sinful anger, pride, and bitterness. The "wood" of the cross was thrown into the bitter waters of my heart. The cross of Jesus humbled me and absorbed all my sin and bitterness (Exodus 15:22-24). Because Jesus loved me through His cross, I am filled with love for Christ and my husband.

God has made me passionate about other people's freedom and healing. I long to see others kneel at the foot of the cross and become awestruck at what Jesus did for them through His death and resurrection. I long to see the spiritual power of the Holy Spirit flow into them as they come to the Rock that was struck and drink from Him (1 Corinthians 10:4).

I still sin and stumble in many ways, but united together with Christ and my husband "*I press on toward the goal to win the prize for which God has called me heavenward in Christ Jesus*" (Philippians 3:14).

Now, I'm eager to hear from you. What changes have you experienced?

Please take your time and share your experience of the past 30 days of walking through these lessons. Did you find hope and healing in Jesus? Did you learn to be a united front with your spouse against the world, the flesh, and the devil? Please share any changes in your life since you started this course.

Question 1: What changes have taken place in your heart and life since you started this study?

Thank you for sharing your testimony. I pray that God will open many doors for you to continue to share it so that many others will desire the transforming power of the gospel in their own lives.

Question 2: Would you recommend this course to others? If yes, what words of encouragement would you offer them? If no, please share why.

_____

_____

_____

_____

Thank you for sharing. I sincerely hope that you have found this study beneficial and that you have become a united front with your spouse.

Please pray for the ministry of Setting Captives Free. We need your prayer support as we share the gospel of Jesus Christ. And we'd love to hear from you at any time; please write in and let us know of any ongoing changes as you continue. You can write to us at helpdesk@settingcaptivesfree.com.

Praying for your Spouse

*J*esus said in Luke 6:27-28 NIV, *"But I say to you who hear, love your enemies, do good to those who hate you, bless those who curse you, pray for those who mistreat you."*

Praying for your spouse who has hurt you can be difficult, but if you want to become a united front with your spouse against the world, the flesh, and the devil, praying for your spouse is critical.

In times of distress, it can be difficult to know what to pray. But the good news is that God has made provision for us in His Word. We can know that we are praying according to the will of God when we are praying God's Word back to Him.

Notice John 15:7-8 (NIV), *"If you remain in me and my words remain in you, ask whatever you wish, and it will be done for you. This is to my Father's glory, that you bear much fruit, showing yourselves to be my disciples."*

> **Question 1:** What are the two requirements for receiving whatever we ask for in prayer?
> - ☐ That we are obedient to the Law and that we walk by the Spirit.
> - ☐ That we remain in Christ and His words remain in us.
> - ☐ That we overcome sin and bear fruit to God's glory.

The truth that we want to see is that we must pray according to God's will, which means praying according to His Word. If we are remaining in Jesus through Bible study and prayer, He will give us His Word to pray back to Him.

If you pray His Word, not taking it out of context, you can "ask whatever you wish, and it will be done for you." This kind of prayer is very exciting.

When we pray God's Word, we know that we are praying in agreement with God, and He will answer us accordingly.

Psalm 107 offers us four descriptive word pictures of people who are in desperate situations like us. These people are in deep trouble, and so they cry out to the Lord, and He rescues and delivers them. Let's use this chapter to facilitate our own praying and see how praying God's Word brings us the assurance that God hears and answers.

First picture: The Wilderness Wanderer

> *Psalms 107:4-9 (NIV) Some wandered in desert wastelands, finding no way to a city where they could settle. They were hungry and thirsty, and their lives ebbed away. Then they cried out to the Lord in their trouble, and he delivered them from their distress. He led them by a straight way to a city where they could settle. Let them give thanks to the Lord for his unfailing love and his wonderful deeds for mankind, for he satisfies the thirsty and fills the hungry with good things.*

Here is the repeating theme of this chapter:

- There are people in a very difficult situation—verses 4-5
- The people cry out to the Lord—verse 6
- God delivers the people from their distress—verse 7
- The people praise and thank God for His love and deliverance—verses 8-9

Here is how you might pray this passage back to God:

> *Father in heaven, like the people in this chapter, my spouse has been wandering in the wilderness of lust unsettled, extremely hungry, and thirsty in sin, deriving no lasting satisfaction from the temporary pleasures of sin.*
>
> *Oh, God, I cry to You now, for I've seen in this passage that You hear the cries of those who are desperate. I'm desperate to help*

my spouse stop this wandering in sin, but I need You to show me how to help my spouse see the "way to the city."

We need You, Lord, to open the eyes of our hearts to see Jesus who, through His death, opened the way for us to come home together to You.

Oh, God, please lead my spouse out of the hot, dry, barren, and arid wasteland of sexual impurity. Please deliver us from our distress! Rescue my spouse from wandering, save me from this desolate place of sadness and despair I've been living in, and lead us both back to You.

I believe You will do this for Your glory, and I will praise You and thank you for it. In Jesus' name, Amen.

Second Picture: The Chained Captive

Psalms 107:10-16 (NIV) Some sat in darkness, in utter darkness, prisoners suffering in iron chains, because they rebelled against God's commands and despised the plans of the Most High. So, he subjected them to bitter labor; they stumbled, and there was no one to help. Then they cried to the Lord in their trouble, and he saved them from their distress. He brought them out of darkness, the utter darkness, and broke away their chains. Let them give thanks to the Lord for his unfailing love and his wonderful deeds for mankind, for he breaks down gates of bronze and cuts through bars of iron.

Now, it's your turn.

Question 2: Please write out your prayer to God using His actual words from Psalm 107:10-16:

_____

_____

_____

_____

Third picture: The Sin-Sick Sufferer

Psalms 107:17-22 (NIV) Some became fools through their rebellious ways and suffered affliction because of their iniquities. They loathed all food and drew near the gates of death. Then they cried to the Lord in their trouble, and he saved them from their distress. He sent out his word and healed them; he rescued them from the grave. Let them give thanks to the Lord for his unfailing love and his wonderful deeds for mankind. Let them sacrifice thank offerings and tell of his works with songs of joy.

We might pray:

Father in heaven, in various ways my spouse and I have behaved foolishly. We have not always lived in Your wisdom. My spouse has lived to gratify the lusts of the flesh, and I have been living in fear and bitterness. We are suffering affliction in our personal life, family life and in many other areas of our lives. We are so sick we can hardly feed on your Word or pray. Our marriage needs Your resurrection power.

I see in your Word that you hear people who cry Your Word out to you. Oh Lord, from the depths of my heart, I ask you to heal me! Oh, Lord, send forth your word and cure me and my spouse! I turn to the cross of Jesus, and as I look up, I see that You did indeed send forth your Word, Your living Word, Jesus. And I remember that by His stripes, I am healed. Oh, Father, I need to see His healing stripes, that is, His death in my place and my spouse's place. We need You to make us well.

Please heal us by Your Word, for Your glory, and I will praise and thank you for it. In Jesus' name, Amen.

Fourth Picture: The Tempest Tossed Traveler

Psalms 107:23-30 (NIV) Some went out on the sea in ships; they were merchants on the mighty waters. They saw the works of the Lord, his wonderful deeds in the deep. For he spoke and stirred up a tempest that lifted high the waves. They mounted up to the heavens and went down to the depths; in their peril, their courage melted away. They reeled and staggered like drunkards; they were at their wits' end. Then they cried out to the Lord in their trouble, and he brought them out of their distress. He stilled the storm to a whisper; the waves of the sea were hushed. They were glad when it grew calm, and he guided them to their desired haven.

Question 3: This is your place to pray God's Word back to Him, believing He will honor His Word and hear your prayer.

Oh, friend, this is how to wrestle with God in prayer for your marriage: take His Word, latch on to it, and pray it back to Him.

The exciting thing is that we have a huge Bible to pray back to God. We can latch onto a verse, passage, even a chapter a day, and wrestle with God in it. God honors His Word and His name (Psalm 138:2). As you begin praying in a believing way, trusting that God will honor His Word at the proper time, you will experience the answers of God. We are praying for you in this.

Blessing Your Spouse
for Jesus' Sake

Romans 12:21 "Do not be overcome by evil but overcome evil with good."

The purpose of this list is to give you a few ideas for how you might bless your spouse. A blessing isn't a blessing if it has an ulterior motive; so, remember we do these things for Jesus' sake not because we are expecting something in return. You should give a blessing not with the motive to produce a change in your spouse or to merit favor with your spouse but simply because it brings glory to God when you do it. Remember that while we were still sinners, Christ died for us, and allow the gospel to spur you on to blessing your spouse for Jesus' sake.

- Speak words that build your spouse up and encourage them in the gospel.
- Do something with your spouse that they enjoy.
- Write a loving note, email or letter to your spouse.
- Flirt with your spouse.
- Make yourself look nice for your spouse.
- Read a Christ-centered book with your spouse.
- Take your spouse on a date—plan everything.
- Help your spouse complete a project that is important to them.
- Try to remove one stressor from your spouse's life.

- Show your spouse affection—hugs, kisses, compliments, etc.
- Show your spouse that you appreciate them.
- Get rid of something that your spouse hates—even if you "love" it (old clothes, shoes, furniture…).
- Buy or make something that your spouse will like or enjoy.
- Write a note of encouragement and put it where your spouse will find it.
- Listen to your spouse—lean forward, make eye contact, be responsive.